Editor
Evan D. Forbes, M.S. Ed.

Editorial Project Manager
Charles Payne, M.A., M.F.A.

Editor in Chief
Sharon Coan, M.S. Ed.

Illustrator
Chandler Sinnott

Photo Cover Credit
Images provided by
PhotoDisc ©1994

Art Coordinator
Denice Adorno

Creative Director
Elayne Roberts

Imaging
Evan D. Forbes, M.S. Ed.

Product Manager
Phil Garcia

Publishers
Rachelle Cracchiolo, M.S. Ed.
Mary Dupuy Smith, M.S. Ed.

Hands-On Minds-On Science

Rain Forest

Primary

Author
Tricia Ball, M.S. Ed.
GATE/Mentor Teacher

Teacher Created Materials, Inc.
6421 Industry Way
Westminster, CA   92683
www.teachercreated.com

ISBN-1-57690-385-0

©2000 Teacher Created Materials, Inc.
Reprinted, 2002
Made in U.S.A.

Table of Contents

Introduction. 4

The Scientific Method. 5

Science-Process Skills 7

Organizing Your Unit 9

What Is a Rain Forest?

Just the Facts 11
Hands-On Activities

 • Locating the Rain Forests 13

 • Big Tree . . .Little Tree 15

 • Measure a Tree 17

 • How Tall Is It? 20

 • Making Rain 23

What Grows in the Tropical Rain Forest?

Just the Facts 25
Hands-On Activities

 • What Is a Bromeliad? 26

 • Growing a Sweet Potato Vine 30

What Lives in the Tropical Rain Forest?

Just the Facts 31
Hands-On Activities

 • Leaping Lizards 32

 • A Fox That Flies? 35

 • Our Fine-Feathered Friends 40

 • Spying on Spiders 41

What Can You Do to Save the Rain Forest?

Just the Facts 44
Hands-On Activities

 • Jungle Journey 45

 • Earth Day Quilt 46

Table of Contents *(cont.)*

What Can You Do to Save the Rain Forest? *(cont.)*

- Countdown to Action to Save Our Earth 47
    - DAY 10 Activity—Chart Your Course 48
    - DAY 9 Activity—Anti-Litter Bugs 49
    - DAY 8 Activity—Supply Spies 50
    - DAY 7 Activity—Plant Power 51
    - DAY 6 Activity—Light the Way 52
    - DAY 5 Activity—Lunch Bunch 53
    - DAY 4 Activity—Waste Watchers 54
    - DAY 3 Activity—Media Mania 56
    - DAY 2 Activity—Check the Chart 57
    - DAY 1 Activity—Blast Off! 58

Station-to-Station Activities

- Observe 59
- Communicate 61
- Compare 62
- Order 63
- Categorize 64
- Relate 65
- Infer 66
- Apply 67

Management Tools

- Animal Information Cards 69
- Animal Illustration Cards 80
- Science Safety 83
- My Rain Forest Journal 84
- My Science Activity 87
- Investigation Planner 88
- Rain Forest Observation Area 89
- Assessment Form 90
- Super Biologist Award 91

Glossary 92

Bibliography 95

Introduction

What Is Science?

What is science to young children? Is it something that they know is a part of their world? Is it a textbook in the classroom? Is it a tadpole changing into a frog? Is it a sprouting seed, a rainy day, a boiling pot, a turning wheel, a pretty rock, or a moonlit sky? Is science fun and filled with wonder and meaning? What is science to children?

Science offers you and your eager students opportunities to explore the world around you and to make connections among the things you experience. The world becomes your classroom, and you, the teacher, a guide.

Science can, and should, fill children with wonder. It should cause them to be filled with questions and the desire to discover the answers to their questions. And, once they have discovered answers, they should be actively seeking new questions to answer.

The books in this series give you and the students in your classroom the opportunity to learn from the whole of your experience—the sights, sounds, smells, tastes, and touches, as well as what you read, write about, and do. This whole-science approach allows you to experience and understand your world as you explore science concepts and skills together.

What Is the Rain Forest?

The tropical rain forest is located near the equator. Tropical rain forests are very special places. Seven percent of the earth's land areas are tropical rain forests. They are warm all year round. The rain forest got its name because it rains every day. Some of these rains can just be showers, or they can be harsh downpours that last a few hours. These hot and humid regions have at least 75 inches (2 m) of rain a year. Temperatures in the rain forest are fairly constant. They range from 68° F (20° C) to 85° F (30° C) both day and night all year long. The days are hot and moist, and the evenings are damp and warm. It rarely gets cool in the evening in tropical the rain forest.

The Scientific Method

The "scientific method" is one of several creative and systematic processes for proving or disproving a given question, following an observation. When the scientific method is used in the classroom, a basic set of guiding principles and procedures is followed in order to answer a question. However, real world science is often not as rigid as the scientific method would have us believe.

This systematic method of problem solving is described in the paragraphs that follow.

1 Make an OBSERVATION.

The teacher presents a situation, gives a demonstration, or reads background material that interests students and prompts them to ask questions. Or students can make observations and generate questions on their own as they study a topic.

2 Select a QUESTION to investigate.

In order for students to select a question for a scientific investigation, they will have to consider the materials they have or can get, as well as the resources (books, magazines, people, etc.) actually available to them. You can help them make an inventory of their materials and resources, either individually or as a group.

Tell students that in order to successfully investigate the questions they have selected, they must be very clear about what they are asking. Discuss effective questions with your students. Depending upon their level, simplify the question or make it more specific.

3 Make a PREDICTION (hypothesis).

Explain to students that a hypothesis is a good guess about what the answer to a question will probably be. But they do not want to make just any arbitrary guess. Encourage students to predict what they think will happen and why.

In order to formulate a hypothesis, students may have to gather more information through research.

Have students practice making hypotheses with questions you give them. Tell them to pretend they have already done their research. You want them to write each hypothesis so it follows these rules:

1. It is to the point.
2. It tells what will happen, based on what the question asks.
3. It follows the subject/verb relationship of the question.

The Scientific Method *(cont.)*

4 Develop a **PROCEDURE** to test the hypothesis.

The first thing students must do in developing a procedure (the test plan) is to determine the materials they will need.

They must state exactly what needs to be done in step-by-step order. If they do not place their directions in the right order, or if they leave out a step, it becomes difficult for someone else to follow their directions. A scientist never knows when other scientists will want to try the same experiment to see if they end up with the same results!

5 Record the **RESULTS** of the investigation in written and picture form.

The results (data collected) of a scientific investigation are usually expressed two ways—in written form and in picture form. Both are summary statements. The written form reports the results with words. The picture form (often a chart or graph) reports the results so the information can be understood at a glance.

6 State a **CONCLUSION** that tells what the results of the investigation mean.

The conclusion is a statement which tells the outcome of the investigation. It is drawn after the student has studied the results of the experiment, and it interprets the results in relation to the stated hypothesis. A conclusion statement may read something like either of the following: "The results show that the hypothesis is supported," or "The results show that the hypothesis is not supported." Then restate the hypothesis if it was supported or revise it if it was not supported.

7 Record **QUESTIONS, OBSERVATIONS**, and **SUGGESTIONS** for future investigations.

Students should be encouraged to reflect on the investigations that they complete. These reflections, like those of professional scientists, may produce questions that will lead to further investigations.

Science-Process Skills

Even the youngest students blossom in their ability to make sense out of their world and succeed in scientific investigations when they learn and use the science-process skills. These are the tools that help children think and act like professional scientists.

The first five process skills on the list below are the ones that should be emphasized with young children, but all of the skills will be utilized by anyone who is involved in scientific study.

Observing

It is through the process of observation that all information is acquired. That makes this skill the most fundamental of all the process skills. Children have been making observations all their lives, but they need to be made aware of how they can use their senses and prior knowledge to gain as much information as possible from each experience. Teachers can develop this skill in children by asking questions and making statements that encourage precise observations.

Communicating

Humans have developed the ability to use language and symbols which allow them to communicate not only in the "here and now" but also over time and space as well. The accumulation of knowledge in science, as in other fields, is due to this process skill. Even young children should be able to understand the importance of researching others' communications about science and the importance of communicating their own findings in ways that are understandable and useful to others. The endangered species journal and the data-capture sheets used in this book are two ways to develop this skill.

Comparing

Once observation skills are heightened, students should begin to notice the relationships among things that they are observing. *Comparing* means noticing similarities and differences. By asking how things are alike and different or which is smaller or larger, teachers will encourage children to develop their comparison skills.

Ordering

Other relationships that students should be encouraged to observe are the linear patterns of seriation (order along a continuum: e.g., rough to smooth, large to small, bright to dim, few to many) and sequence (order along a time line or cycle). By ranking graphs, time lines, cyclical and sequence drawings and by putting many objects in order by a variety of properties, students will grow in their abilities to make precise observations about the order of nature.

Categorizing

When students group or classify objects or events according to logical rationale, they are using the process skill of categorizing. Students begin to use this skill when they group by a single property such as color. As they develop this skill, they will be attending to multiple properties in order to make categorizations; the animal classification system, for example, is one system students can categorize.

Science-Process Skills *(cont.)*

Relating
Relating, which is one of the higher-level process skills, requires student scientists to notice how objects and phenomena interact with one another and the changes caused by these interactions. An obvious example of this is the study of chemical reactions.

Inferring
Not all phenomena are directly observable, because they are out of humankind's reach in terms of time, scale, and space. Some scientific knowledge must be logically inferred based on the data that is available. Much of the work of paleontologists, astronomers, and those studying the structure of matter is done by inference.

Applying
Even very young, budding scientists should begin to understand that people have used scientific knowledge in practical ways to change and improve the way we live. It is at this application level that science becomes meaningful for many students.

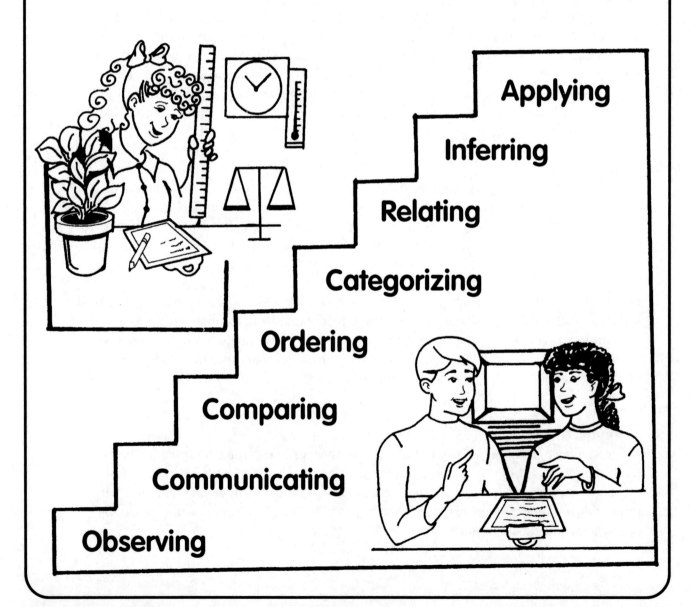

Applying

Inferring

Relating

Categorizing

Ordering

Comparing

Communicating

Observing

Organizing Your Unit

Designing a Science Lesson

In addition to the lessons presented in this unit, you will want to add lessons of your own, lessons that reflect the unique environment in which you live, as well as the interests of your students. When designing new lessons or revising old ones, try to include the following elements in your planning:

Question

Pose a question to your students that will guide them in the direction of the experiment you wish to perform. Encourage all answers, but you want to lead the students towards the experiment you are going to be doing. Remember, there must be an observation before there can be a question. (Refer to The Scientific Method, pages 5–6.)

Setting the Stage

Prepare your students for the lesson. Brainstorm to find out what students already know. Have children review books to discover what is already known about the subject. Invite them to share what they have learned.

Materials Needed for Each Group or Individual

List the materials each group or individual will need for the investigation. Include a data-capture sheet when appropriate.

Procedure

Make sure students know the steps to take to complete the activity. Whenever possible, ask them to determine the procedure. Make use of assigned roles in group work. Create (or have your students create) a data-capture sheet. Ask yourself, "How will my students record and report what they have discovered? Will they tally, measure, draw, or make a checklist? Will they make a graph? Will they need to preserve specimens?" Let students record results orally, using a videotape or audiotape recorder. For written recording, encourage students to use a variety of paper supplies such as poster board or index cards. It is also important for students to each keep a journal of their investigation activities. Journals can be made of lined and unlined paper. Students can design their own covers. The pages can be stapled or be put together with brads or spiral binding.

Extensions

Continue the success of the lesson. Consider which related skills or information you can tie into the lesson, like math, language arts skills, or something being learned in social studies. Make curriculum connections frequently and involve the students in making these connections. Extend the activity, whenever possible, to home investigations.

Closure

Encourage students to think about what they have learned and how the information connects to their own lives. Prepare endangered species journals using directions on page 84. Provide an ample supply of blank and lined pages for students to use as they complete the "Closure" activities. Allow time for students to record their thoughts and pictures in their journals.

Organizing Your Unit *(cont.)*

Structuring Student Groups for Scientific Investigations

Using cooperative learning strategies in conjunction with hands-on and discovery learning methods will benefit all the students taking part in the investigation.

Cooperative Learning Strategies

1. In cooperative learning, all group members need to work together to accomplish the task.
2. Cooperative learning groups should be heterogeneous.
3. Cooperative learning activities need to be designed so that each student contributes to the group and individual group members can be assessed on their performance.
4. Cooperative learning teams need to know the social as well as the academic objectives of a lesson.

Cooperative Learning Groups

Groups can be determined many ways for the scientific investigations in your class. Here is one way of forming groups that has proven to be successful in primary classrooms.

- **The Team Leader**—scientist in charge of reading directions and setting up equipment.
- **The Biologist**—scientist in charge of carrying out directions (can be more than one student).
- **The Stenographer**—scientist in charge of recording all of the information.
- **The Transcriber**—scientist who translates notes and communicates findings.

If the groups remain the same for more than one investigation, require each group to vary the people chosen for each job. All group members should get a chance to try each job at least once.

Using Centers for Scientific Investigations

Set up stations for each investigation. To accommodate several groups at a time, stations may be duplicated for the same investigation. Each station should contain directions for the activity, all necessary materials (or a list of materials for investigators to gather), a list of words (a word bank) which students may need for writing and speaking about the experience, and any data-capture sheets or needed materials for recording and reporting data and findings.

Station-to-Station Activities are on pages 59–68. Model and demonstrate each of the activities for the whole group. Have directions at each station. During the modeling session, have a student read the directions aloud while the teacher carries out the activity. When all students understand what they must do, let small groups conduct the investigations at the centers. You may wish to have a few groups working at the centers while others are occupied with other activities. In this case, you will want to set up a rotation schedule so all groups have a chance to work at the centers.

Assign each team to a station, and after they complete the task described, help them rotate in a clockwise order to the other stations. If some groups finish earlier than others, be prepared with another unit-related activity to keep students focused on main concepts. After all rotations have been made by all groups, come together as a class to discuss what was learned.

Just the Facts

The rain forest is a very special place. It is home to a large number of plants and animals. Close your eyes and listen to the sounds of the rain forest. It is very quiet on the forest floor. Above your head, you can hear the faint songs of the birds, the chirps of the insects, the howls and the chatter of the monkeys. You can feel the hot, moist air surrounding you and feel the soft, steady rain falling on your face. Tropical rain forests are beautiful and mysterious places.

The rain forest covers only about seven percent of the Earth's land. You can find a rain forest in many countries that are located in an area known as the tropics. The tropics is an area found between the Tropic of Cancer and the Tropic of Capricorn. In the center of the tropics is the equator, the imaginary line that divides the Earth into two hemispheres. There are rain forests in India, Southeast Asia, Australia, the East and West Indies, Malaysia, the Philippines, Central and South America and even in parts of Washington state and Florida, but the largest remaining tropical rain forest is located in the Amazon River Basin of South America.

The temperature in the rain forest is fairly constant, usually between 68° and 85° F (20° and 30° C) both day and night all year long. Humidity is very high. Most days it ranges between 75 and 100 percent.

In addition to the tropical rain forest, there are several other types of rain forest. There is the temperate rain forest. The temperate rain forest is cooler and does not have the vast variety of plants and animals the tropical rain forest has. There is the monsoon rain forest. This rain forest has a wet and dry season, and the plants are not as dense. Finally, there is the montane rain forest. The montane rain forests are high altitude forests with a wide range of temperatures. They can be found in Central and South America, as well as in Central Africa and New Guinea.

Every rain forest has various strata or layers of plants. The rain forest has four main strata. They are, from the highest to the lowest, (1) the emergent layer, (2) the canopy, (3) the understory, and (4) the forest floor.

The Emergent Layer

The emergent layer is the highest layer in the rain forest. This layer is exposed to the sun and is the home for many birds of prey. The trees in the emergent layer can grow to a height of more than 300 feet (91 m). The emergent layer and the canopy are a huge food-making factory where most of the forest's photosynthesis takes place.

Just the Facts *(cont.)*

The Canopy

Below the emergent layer is a second layer. It consists mainly of the crowns (branches and leaves) of the tallest trees. Trees in the canopy are about 150 to 250 feet (46 m to 76 m) tall and are home to many birds and animals. The canopy receives full sunlight and produces more food than any other layer.

The Understory

Beneath the canopy is the understory. The understory receives only one percent of the sunlight in the forest. It is dim and humid. There are vines, bushes, shrubs, and small trees growing in the understory. A special type of plant called the epiphyte grows in the understory. The epiphytes are plants that live on other plants for support but absorb from the air the water and other materials they need for food.

The Forest Floor

The lowest layer of the forest is the floor. The floor is very dim and almost no light gets through the upper layers to light it. There is also very little wind. Even during the most violent rainstorms, the thickness of the plant growth reduces the wind so that the floor remains calm. Few plants grow on the forest floor, and except for the trunks of the tall trees, the floor is very open.

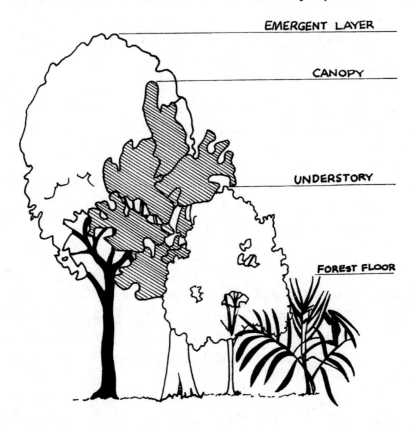

EMERGENT LAYER

CANOPY

UNDERSTORY

FOREST FLOOR

12

Locating the Rain Forests

Question

Can you find and label all the rain forests on the map of the world?

Setting the Stage

On a wall or overhead map locate and discuss the areas that contain the world's rain forests. Have the students locate the Tropic of Cancer and the Tropic of Capricorn. Discuss the type of climates found in these areas and elicit from the class what continents and countries are located there.

Materials Needed for Each Individual

- crayons or colored pencils
- pencil
- a copy of "Locating the Rain Forests" (page 14)
- world map or an atlas

Procedure

1. After the class discussion, distribute a copy of the work sheet to each student.
2. Have each student label and color the areas of the world rain forests on his/her map.
3. Paste the completed maps into their rain forest journals.

Extensions

- Depending upon the level of your students, you might want to use this opportunity to discuss latitude and longitude and do map skill work.
- You may also have the students cut pictures out of magazines or draw pictures of some of the animals or plants that live in the rain forest.

Closure

Creative Writing Journal Entry: How would your life be different if you lived in the rain forest? Draw a picture of you in the jungle.

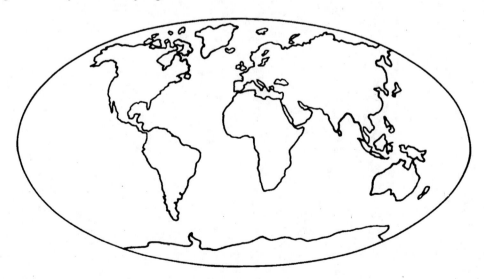

Locating the Rain Forests *(cont.)*

Directions: Use the map below to help you locate and label the following places and then using the same map, locate the world's rain forests.

Tropic of Cancer, Tropic of Capricorn, Equator, Amazon River, Congo River, Africa, Atlantic Ocean, Pacific Ocean, Central America, South America, North America, India, Southeast Asia, West Indies, and East Indies

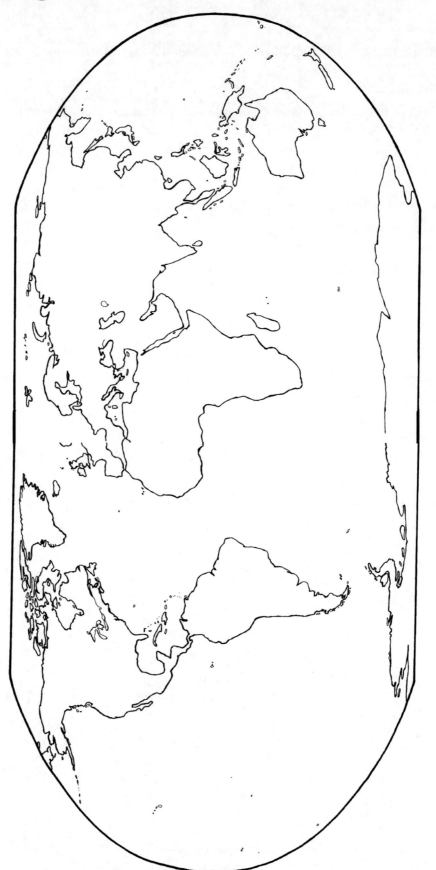

14

Big Tree . . . Little Tree . . .

Question

How big are the trees in the rain forest?

Setting the Stage

Discuss with the class the sizes of the trees and the density of the growth in the rain forest. Have on hand many books and pictures of the rain forests for the class to observe. It is quite difficult for young students to realize just how big the trees and foliage are in the rain forest, so creating a rain forest in the corner of your room will aid them.

Materials Needed for the Class

- large pieces of brown and green butcher paper
- masking tape
- staple gun, if available
- stapler
- glue
- invisible fishing line

Procedure

1. Choose a large corner of the classroom. Corners work best because you have two walls to use to secure the leaves to the tree.
2. From the brown butcher paper, construct the trunk of your tree by twisting and folding the paper into a wide, firm trunk that reaches to the ceiling of your classroom.
3. Secure the trunk to the ceiling with the staple gun. Masking tape can be used to secure the tree to the floor.
4. Use the twisting and folding method to make branches for your tree. Secure the branches to the tree with staples and to the ceiling with staples, suspending the arms of the branches with fishing line. It is important that the branches of the tree extend well into the classroom so that the students are given the feeling of being in the rain forest.
5. Construct large green leaves from the remaining butcher paper and attach these leaves to the branches of the tree. Remember to make these leaves large enough to hang down over the children's heads and dense enough to recreate the jungle atmosphere.
6. Put books, pictures, and magazines about the rain forest under the tree. Rain forest sounds on tape can be played in the corner to give authenticity to the corner.

Extensions

- The rain forest tree can be used for a variety of activities. It makes a great writing corner. The atmosphere allows the students' imaginations to go "wild."
- You can leave your tree up throughout the school year and change the leaves for the seasons or for other areas of study.

Big Tree . . . Little Tree . . . *(cont.)*

Closure

- Have the children bring stuffed animals from home or pictures of animals that might live in the rain forest and display them in and under your tree.

- Use the tree as a quiet reading spot to learn more about the rain forest. Select from the books in the bibliography.

Measure a Tree

Question

How can scientists measure the height of a rain forest tree?

Setting the Stage

- Elicit from the students how they might go about measuring the heights of the trees in the rain forests. How do they think scientists do this? Accept all reasonable answers for this discussion.
- Explain to your students what a Luneometer is.
- Then ask them if they can measure the heights of the trees outside your classroom. After they answer, tell them that they are going to measure the heights of the trees outside.

Materials Needed for Each Individual

- a copy of the "Measure a Tree" activity work sheets (pages 18–19)
- scissors
- 8' x 8' (2.4 m x 2.4 m) piece of tagboard
- crayons
- 8' (2.4 m) of string
- one penny

Procedure

1. Glue the luneometer (page 21) to the piece of tagboard.
2. Cut out the luneometer.
3. Glue a folded piece of paper to the back of the top strip of paper on your luneometer.
4. Carefully punch a small hole in the space indicated and thread the string through the hole.
5. Tape the penny to the end if the string and allow it to swing freely.
6. Take your finished luneometer outside and find a tall tree to measure.
7. Hold the luneometer up to your eye and sight along the top edge until you see the top of the tree. Have a friend read the degrees on the luneometer.
8. Find the height of the tree by locating the degrees on the chart and comparing them to the height in meters.

Extension

Use the luneometer to measure various items found outside. A lightpole, the flagpole, and the height of the building are a few examples. The students will come up with many of their own ideas.

Closure

Luneometers are really chronometers. Many scientists, surveyors, and sailors use a similar device to measure the height of things. Have the students research the chronometer and write about its various uses in their journals.

Measure a Tree *(cont.)*

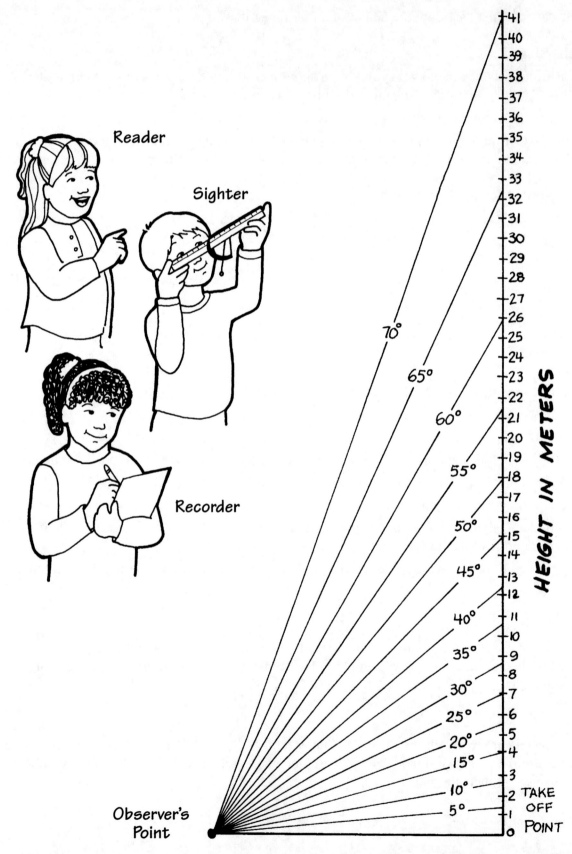

Reader

Sighter

Recorder

70°

65°

60°

55°

50°

45°

40°

35°

30°

25°

20°

15°

10°

5°

Observer's Point

TAKE OFF POINT

HEIGHT IN METERS

41
40
39
38
37
36
35
34
33
32
31
30
29
28
27
26
25
24
23
22
21
20
19
18
17
16
15
14
13
12
11
10
9
8
7
6
5
4
3
2
1
0

Measure a Tree *(cont.)*

Tangent of Angle

Angle°	Tangent	Angle°	Tangent	Angle°	Tangent
1	.01746	31	.6009	61	1.804
2	.03492	32	.6249	62	1.881
3	.05241	33	.6494	63	1.963
4	.06993	34	.6745	64	2.050
5	.08749	35	.7002	65	2.145
6	.10510	36	.7265	66	2.246
7	.12278	37	.7536	67	2.356
8	.14054	38	.7813	68	2.475
9	.15838	39	.8098	69	2.605
10	.1763	40	.8391	70	2.747
11	.1944	41	.8693	71	2.904
12	.2126	42	.9004	72	3.078
13	.2309	43	.9325	73	3.271
14	.2493	44	.9657	74	3.487
15	.2679	45	1.0000	75	3.732
16	.2867	46	1.0355	76	4.011
17	.3057	47	1.0724	77	4.331
18	.3249	48	1.1106	78	4.705
19	.3443	49	1.1504	79	5.145
20	.3640	50	1.1918	80	5.671
21	.3839	51	1.2349	81	6.314
22	.4040	52	1.2799	82	7.115
23	.4245	53	1.3270	83	8.144
24	.4452	54	1.3764	84	9.514
25	.4663	55	1.4281	85	11.430
26	.4877	56	1.4826	86	14.301
27	.5095	57	1.5399	87	19.081
28	.5317	58	1.6003	88	28.64
29	.5543	59	1.6643	89	57.29
30	.5774	60	1.7321	90	——

Tangent of Angle x Distance from Tree = Height

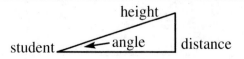

How Tall Is It?

Question

How tall are the trees in your neighborhood?

Setting the Stage

After completing the "Measure a Tree" exercise, ask the students if they can guess how tall the tallest tree on the schoolyard, the flagpole, or the tallest building in the area is. Accept all reasonable answers and then have the students use their luneometers to complete the chart on the following page.

Materials Needed for Each Individual

- luneometer (page 21)
- copy of the "How Tall Is It?" work sheet (page 22)

Procedure

1. Working in pairs, the students sight and measure various tall objects in the schoolyard or around their homes.
2. Record the results on the work sheet.

Extension

The "How Tall Is It?" work sheet can be used to reinforce geometry skills of line and angle. It may also be turned into a math lesson. Numbers in columns can be added, totals can be subtracted, and the work sheet itself uses multiplication.

Closure

This activity may be utilized as a classroom contest with the winning team finding the tallest object in the neighborhood. The object can be a tree, a building, or silo. A small prize for the winners always makes this an exciting activity.

How Tall Is It? *(cont.)*

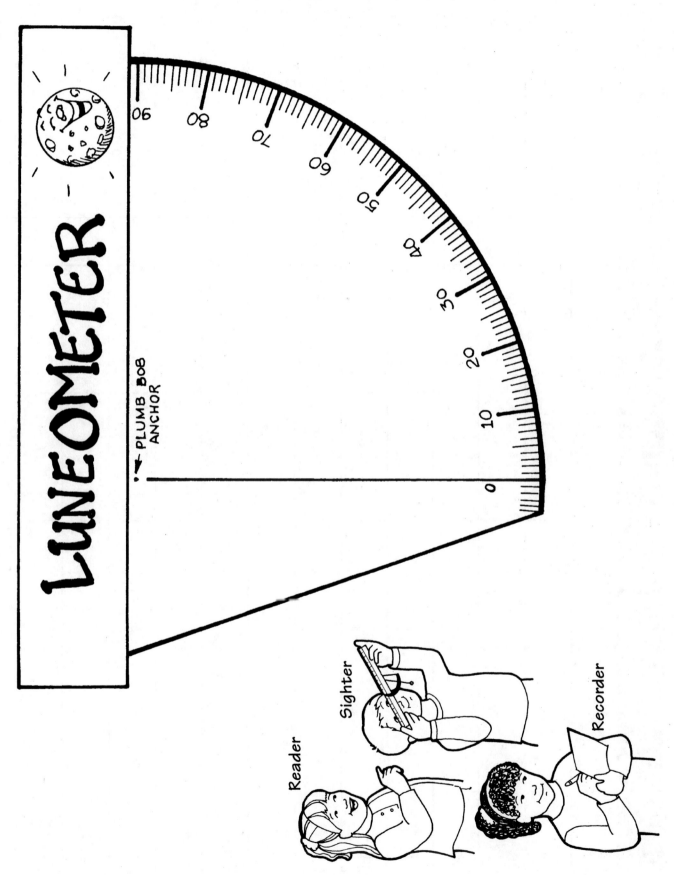

How Tall Is It? *(cont.)*

Name of Object	Estimate of Object's Height	Angle	Tangent of Angle	Distance from Object	Height of Object
1.				m	m
2.				m	m
3.				m	m
4.				m	m
5.				m	m
6.				m	m
7.				m	m
8.				m	m
9.				m	m
10.				m	m
11.				m	m
12.				m	m
13.				m	m

Making Rain

Question

Why does it rain almost every day in the rain forest?

Setting the Stage

Pose the above question to your students. Write all their responses on the board. Try to elicit from them their ideas about how it rains. Some students might respond that rain comes from the clouds or that the clouds make the rain. Then ask, "How do the clouds make rain?" Complete this discussion by doing the making rain demonstration.

Materials Needed for the Teacher

- double boiler
- hot plate or stove
- water
- ice cubes

Procedure

1. Put water in the lower section of the double boiler.
2. Place plenty of water and ice cubes in the upper section.
3. Heat the water in the lower section to a boil.
4. Place the upper section over the lower section of the double boiler.
5. The steam coming from the lower section of boiling water is cooled by the cold surface of the upper section.
6. The steam changes back into water which collects in drops.
7. As the drops get bigger and heavier, they fall down as rain.

Explanation of Demonstration

The boiling water represents the surface of water heated by the sun. The steam is the water that evaporates into the air as water vapor. As the vapor rises, it is cooled. When the conditions are right, droplets form which you see as clouds. As the droplets collect more moisture and become heavier, they finally have enough weight to cause them to fall back to the ground.

8. Have students complete the "Making Rain" observation sheet in their journals.

Making Rain *(cont.)*

Extensions

- Have the class keep a weather log of the daily weather in your local area. Record the humidity levels and have the class predict if it is humid enough to rain. If not, why? Students can make entries into their journals for each day's weather report or keep a record on a large chart in your room.

- Have the class learn about the different types of clouds. Have them draw the cloud shapes for rainy weather, dry weather, stormy weather, etc.

Closure

Using an overhead projector, draw the world map on a large-sized piece of butcher paper. Use yarn or string to locate the world's rain forests. Label the countries and the continents.

24

Just the Facts

The tropical rain forest is home to more than just giant trees. The diversity of plant life in the jungle is higher than in any other habitat in the world. The jungles of the Amazon rain forest in South America are home to more than 40,000 species (types) of plants, many of them still not studied.

Although the single most distinguishing characteristic of the rain forest is its thick growth of tall trees, there are many species of plants that are not trees. Epiphytes, or air plants, live on tree trunks or branches and never touch the ground their entire lives. Thousands of epiphytes obtain the nutrients they need directly from the sunlight and the rainfall. Some species of ferns (staghorn), bromeliads, and orchids are just a few rain forest plants.

The dense jungle is also home to numerous species of vines that have adjusted to the sparse sunlight. The largely wooden species are called lianas. Lianas cover the trees and extract nutrients directly from them.

But exotic and rare species of plants are not the only plants in the rain forest. One of the most widely known plants is the banana tree. These trees provide people with their delicious fruit and are also a source of food for the animals that live in the rain forest.

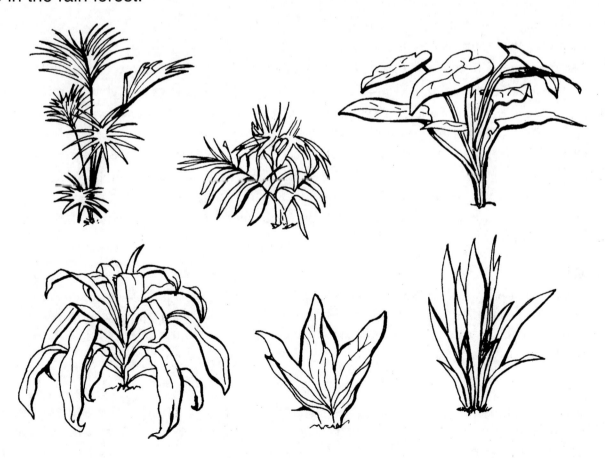

What Is a Bromeliad?

Question

How can you grow a plant in the air?

Setting the Stage

- Elicit from the class the things a plant needs to live and grow. Nutrients, water, sunlight, and soil are important answers. Then ask your students if they think a plant would live on just air. Have them speculate what a plant that lives on just air might look like. You can have the children draw pictures of their plants and have them explain how their plants might function. Then ask if anyone has ever heard of a bromeliad or a staghorn fern? If no one has, explain that a bromeliad is a rare and special type of plant that lives on the air, sunlight, and rain water in the rain forest.

- Bromeliads are relatives of the pineapple. Their cup-shaped leaves sit on branches and catch rain water for the plant. Bromeliads are also home for many of the smaller animals and insects of the rain forest. Worms, beetles, salamanders, and frogs are just a few examples. Even some frogs deposit their tadpoles in the cups of the bromeliad plant.

Materials Needed for Each Individual, Group, or Class (teacher option based on funding)

- bromeliad for each student
- bromeliad work sheets for each student in the class regardless of the number of plants used (pages 27–29)
- hand lenses or microscopes (optional)

Procedure

1. Distribute the bromeliads to the students.
2. Ask the students to carefully observe the plant and record their observations on the work sheets.
3. Point out the formation of the leaves and how they form bulbs or bowls to catch the rain water.
4. Have the students break a leaf from the plant and cut the leaf carefully lengthwise and peel it open. Record observations on work sheets.
5. Observe the leaf under a hand lens or a microscope and draw a picture of the cell structure.
6. Place the plants in a warm, moist area of the classroom. Make sure the sunlight is filtered and not directly on your plant, or it will become too hot and die.
7. Observe the growth of the plant over the length of the unit, and upon completion send the plants home with the children.

Extension

A rain forest picture book can be made from pictures of rain forest plants cut from magazines or drawn by the children. Make this book 18" x 20" (45 cm x 50 cm), using butcher paper. Children love the big size of the book and often equate its size to that of the trees in the rain forest.

Closure

In your rain forest journal, do the following creative writing assignment. "I am a bromeliad. I am home to many animals." Complete the story of your bromeliad and the animal it is home for. Be as creative as you can.

What Is a Bromeliad? *(cont.)*

I am a bromeliad Watch me grow. What do I look like?

Describe the leaves and flowers of your bromeliad.

_____

_____

_____

_____

_____

_____

Draw a picture of your bromeliad.

What Is a Bromeliad? *(cont.)*

Leaf Observation

Draw a picture of your leaf cutting.

Describe how your leaf cutting looks and feels.

_____

_____

_____

_____

_____

Carefully cut the leaf lengthwise and peel it open.

Describe your observations.

_____

_____

_____

_____

_____

What Is a Bromeliad? *(cont.)*

Hand Lens/Microscope Observations

(**Note:** Teachers should be aware that some prior knowledge of plant cells is necessary for this observation.)

Draw a picture of what you see. Identify the plant cell and draw a picture of it.

Growing a Sweet Potato Vine

Question

How do the vines in the rain forest grow and climb trees to obtain sunlight?

Setting the Stage

Discuss the types of vines that entwine themselves in the trees of the rain forest. The story of *Tarzan*, the *Jungle Boy* or *The Jungle Book* may be read to set the scene of the jungle for the students. Then ask if anyone can explain how the vines that Tarzan swung on or that the monkeys play on grow. Accept any reasonable answers. Elicit from the class whether they would like to grow vines in the classroom jungle. The excitement of the jungle is the incentive for this project.

Materials Needed for Each Individual

- plastic drinking cup
- water
- sweet potato (This may be cut into pieces, thus providing a plant for every student, or students may each grow their own potato.)
- toothpicks four, per potato
- sunny location

Procedure

1. Fill the drinking cups halfway with water.
2. Carefully push a toothpick into the middle of each of the four sides of the potato.
3. Place the potato eyes down into the water and set it in a sunny window.

After a few weeks the children will see roots forming on the bottom of the potato and leaves and vines appearing on the top. If left growing over a long period of time, the vines will climb on the walls and cabinets to reach the sun. Remember to maintain the water level in the cups.

Extensions

- Other types of vines may be substituted for the sweet potato. Ivy and other climbing vines work equally as well.
- Make a paper leaf vine. Have the students trace and cut the leaves out of green construction paper. Staple the leaves to string or green yarn and hang them across the ceiling of the classroom. The addition of the vines to the trees really recreates the rain forest for your class.

Closure

In their rain forest journals, have students write about the following: What effects do you think the vines have on the trees and other plants in the rain forest?

Just the Facts

There is an extraordinary number of different animals living in the rain forest. They can be found in all the layers of the forest and depend upon the forest for their food, shelter, and protection. In fact, many of the jungle plants depend upon these animals for pollination, seed dispersal, and even protection. The bats, for example, obtain nectar from flowers for their food. At the same time they are helping to pollinate that same plant. The relationship where one species helps another to survive is called mutualism.

Animal species in the rain forest are just as diverse as the plant life. The largest group of animal life is the insects. Beetles, butterflies, spiders, centipedes, scorpions, and other arthropods make this group the most numerous and diverse group in the tropics. Many new species are being found each year to add to their numbers. There is an ant that builds high anthills in Africa. People use the clay mud from these anthills to make bricks for their houses. Most of the insects in the rain forest are not as helpful as the ant. The anopheles mosquito is a carrier of a disease called malaria, and the tsetse fly is responsible for sleeping sickness.

Another large population of animal in the rain forest is the reptiles. The largest snakes on Earth, the pythons of the Old World and the anacondas of South America, are found in the rain forest. Lizards are also abundant in the forest. You can see many species warming themselves in the high branches of the trees during the day. Also amphibians, such as frogs and salamanders, are common tropical inhabitants.

Of all the diverse animal life found in the rain forest, the mammals are the most well known. When most people think of the jungle, they think of monkeys and gorillas swinging from vines in the trees, but the tropics are home to more species of bats than any other mammal. These bats are an extremely important factor in the rain forests' regrowth today.

Bird diversity is also abundant in the tropics. Many of these species include the most colorful of all the birds in the world. They include the parrots, macaws, birds of paradise, and even the parakeet. The jungles of South America are mainly inhabited by birds of prey such as the harpy eagle and the African crowned eagle.

Leaping Lizards

Question

What reptile found in the rain forest flies?

Setting the Stage

- Ask the students if they know the answer to the question. Allow time for all reasonable answers. Discuss the physical structure of the birds that fly, wings, etc. Then explain that there are some animals in the rain forest that do not really fly like birds but glide or leap from tree to tree. In fact, there are many animals that live their entire lives in the treetops of the rain forest.
- **Flying Dragons:** The flying dragon lives on insects in the rain forests of Asia. Flying dragons are not the dragons that breathe fire and smoke, but lizards. They have extra flaps of skin along the sides of their bodies that help them glide.
- **Flying Snakes:** These unusual Southeast Asian snakes feed on lizards. They are able to spread their ribs and flatten their bodies to become flyers.

Materials Needed for Each Individual

- copy of the Leaping Lizards activity sheets (pages 32–34)
- crayons or markers
- scissors
- paper clips

Procedure

1. Color the lizard and the tail on page 34. Then cut them out along the thick, solid black lines.

2. Lay the paper down with the lizard side facing you and fold along line A so that the drawing "disappears." Make a crease.

3. Unfold the glider, turn it over (lizard side down), and fold back along the B lines. (The two number 1s should meet on the backside of the glider, along the crease made in step 2.)

4. Without unfolding step 3, fold back along line C. (The point labeled 2 should meet the two number 1 corners.)

Leaping Lizards *(cont.)*

5. Turn the glider over so that the lizard side is facing you again. Refold along line A. (You should not be able to see the lizard anymore.)

6. Lay the glider down on its side so that the "open" side faces you. (The crease should be facing away from you.)

7. Slowly lift up the top sheet and fold back along line D.

8. Fold the other side of the glider back.

9. Use a small piece of tape to attach the tail to the lizard where the Ds meet.

10. Cut along the E—underneath the nose of the glider—and then tape the loose pieces in place.

11. Attach a large paper clip to the underside of the glider at the asterisks (*). (You may need to move the paper clip up or down to improve the lizard's flight.)

12. Hold along the bottom crease where line E, the 2, and the 1s meet.

    Now launch your gliding lizard and watch it sail!

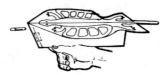

Extension

There are many other unusual animals that live in the rain forest. Have the students research the sloths that have claws to help them hold tight to tree branches; the iguana, the vegetarian lizards that make the canopy their home; the tamanduas, the anteaters that use their tails to hold onto branches of the trees; and the tarsiers, which have friction pads on the ends of their toes that help them grab onto trees and branches.

Closure

- After completing the Leaping Lizard activity, have the students fly their lizards outdoors. Measurements can be made of whose lizard flew the farthest or the highest.

- In their rain forest journals, have students write an adventure story about a child in the rain forest and the unusual animals he/she meets.

Leaping Lizards *(cont.)*

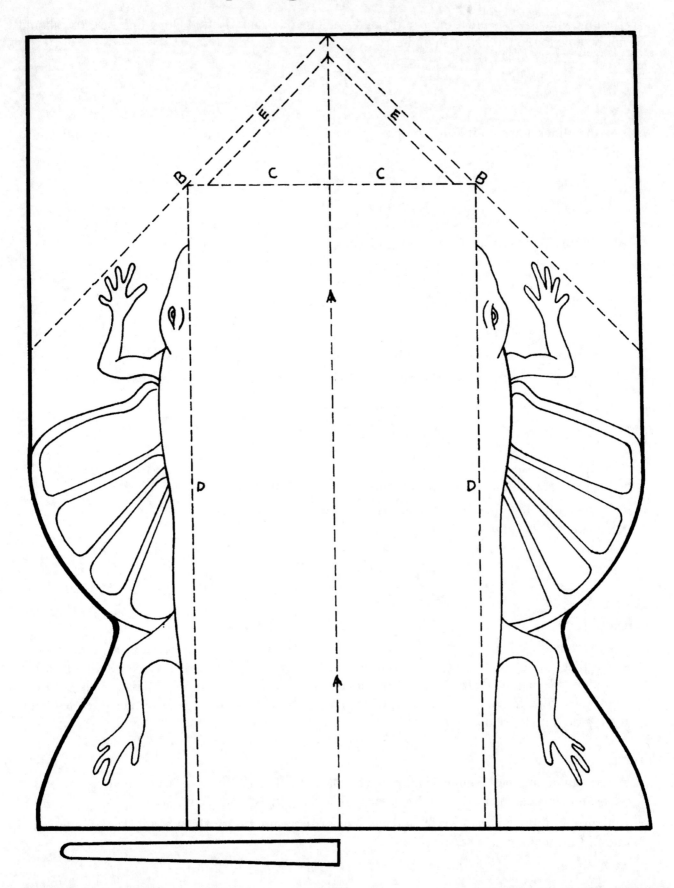

A Fox That Flies?

Question

What animal in the rain forest looks like a fox and flies?

Setting the Stage

- Pose the above question to your students. Accept all reasonable answers. It might be that someone might put it together with the right answer, the flying fox. The flying fox is really one of the largest bats in the world. It is called a flying fox because it flies, and it has a face like a bat. Some of these bats' wingspans stretch nearly six feet (1.8 m).

- Many of these flying foxes live in Southeast Asia, Africa, and Australia and on islands in the South Pacific. There are more than 30 different species of flying foxes.

- The flying fox differs from other bats which eat insects; they eat fruit, nectar, and pollen. Another way these bats differ from their relatives is that they use their keen eyesight to help them find food instead of echolocation.

- These giant bats help reforest the rain forest by spreading seeds and pollinating flowers. They are endangered species in some of the areas in which they live.

Materials Needed for Each Individual

- copy of the patterns on pages 37–39
- tagboard or poster board
- glue
- pencil
- string
- ruler
- craft stick
- scissors
- tape
- pushpin
- markers, crayons, or paint and paintbrush

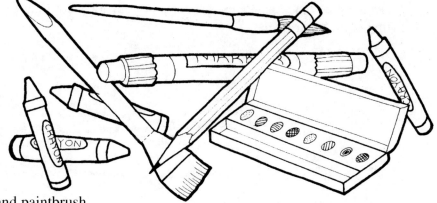

Procedure

1. Cut out the patterns for the bat's body and wings. Trace two of each pattern onto your tag/poster board and cut them out.
2. Draw a line along the bottom of each wing, about one-half inch from the edge.
3. Score along the lines and then bend these tabs back and forth.
4. Cut 18 half-inch (1.25 cm) squares.
5. On one piece of the bat's body, glue a tag/poster board square to each of the six places marked by stars. See pattern.
6. Glue two more squares on top of these. (three squares thick)
7. Glue the craft stick onto the body and let dry.
8. Cut an 18-inch (45 cm) piece of string and lay it across the body between the four middle squares as shown on pattern. Let dry.

A Fox That Flies? *(cont.)*

9. Put a dot of glue on each of the squares and on the craft stick and place the two halves of the bat's body together making sure the halves line up and the string is between the halves.

10. To attach the wings, lay the bat on its side and with the wing up. Glue the tab onto the body, about one-half inch from the top of the back and tape over the tab to secure.

11. Fold the wing down and reinforce it with tape.

12. Using the pushpin, make a hole in the wings where indicated.

13. Cut an 8-inch (20 cm) piece of string and thread the ends through the holes on top of the wings. Tape about one-half inch (1.25 cm) of string to the underside of each wing.

14. Tie the string running through the middle of the bat's body to the center of the string connecting the wings.

15. Use markers, crayons, or paints to color the flying fox.

16. Hold the craft stick and pull the bottom of the long string to make the bat flap its wings.

Extensions

- Find out more about bats. Read some of the suggested books in the bibliography.
- Have the students make a chart of the different species of bats and chart their differences.

Closure

Make a list of other endangered species in your journal. Find pictures in magazines and paste them next to their names.

A Fox That Flies? *(cont.)*

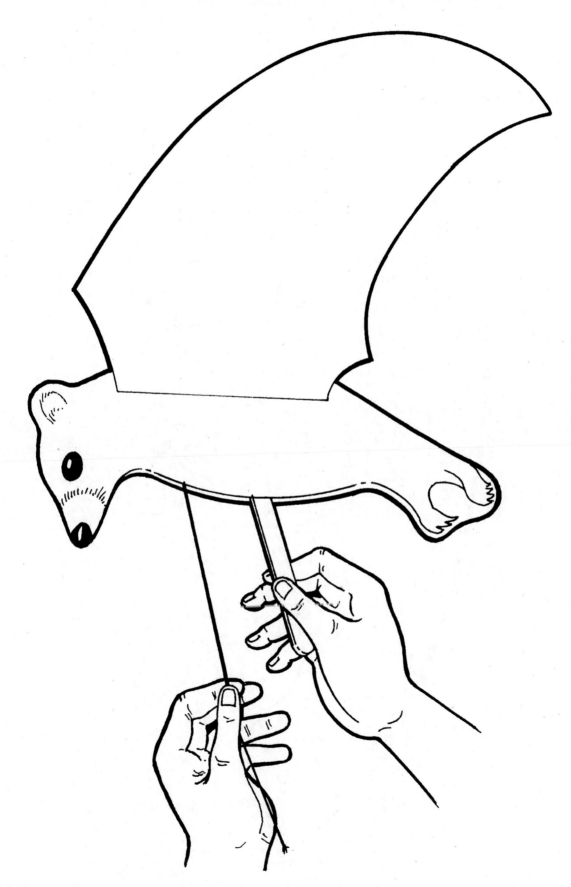

A Fox That Flies? *(cont.)*

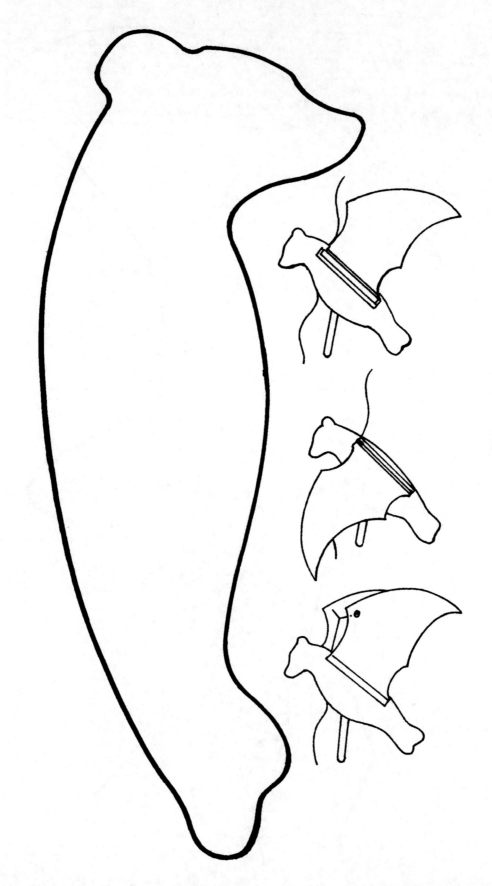

A Fox That Flies? *(cont.)*

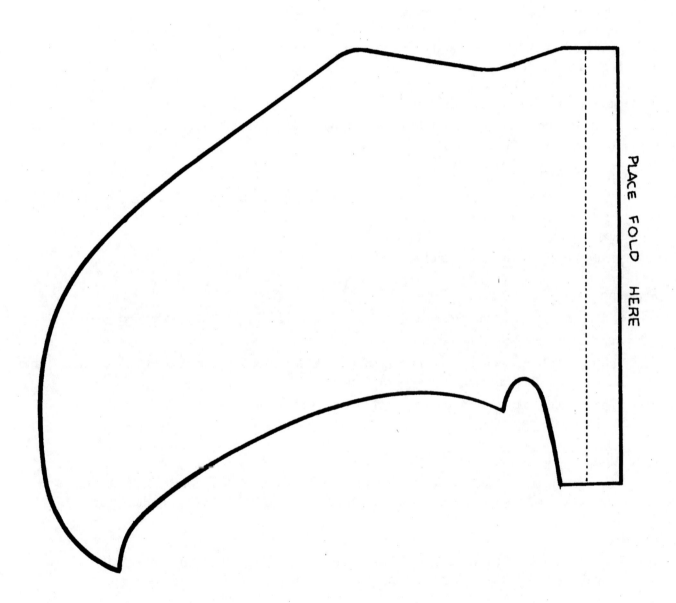

PLACE FOLD HERE

Our Fine-Feathered Friends

Question

How can we help the birds in the rain forest by recycling?

Setting the Stage

Most children have some knowledge about recycling. Assess their knowledge and have them make suggestions about how we could reuse the materials we recycle. Ask the students how they think we can help the birds, not only in the rain forest but right at home. Accept all reasonable suggestions. Hold up the plastic pantihose egg and have them make suggestions on how it might be reused. Then explain that they are going to recycle while making a "Fine-Feathered Friend."

Materials Needed for Each Individual

- plastic pantyhose egg (White or black is best, but any color can be used because the birds in the rain forest are so colorful.)
- modeling clay
- scissors
- construction paper
- tape or glue
- pictures of the birds in the rain forest

Procedure

1. Open the plastic egg and press a golf-ball-sized lump of clay into the smaller half.
2. Put the egg together. If it does not stand upright, reposition the clay.
3. Have the children search through books and magazines for a bird they would like to make. Have them draw wings, beaks, and feet for their bird.
4. Tape or glue the cutouts onto the egg. If glue is used, it should be tacky before you press the parts onto the egg.

Extension

The same materials may be used for other animals found in the rain forest. Just have the students find pictures of animals they like and draw the parts. Then paste them onto the egg.

Closure

Have the students each write a story about their feathered friend in their journals. It can be a factual story about the animals' habitat or a creative tale.

Spying on Spiders

Question

How do scientists in the rain forest learn more about the creatures that live there?

Setting the Stage

Explain to the students that today they are going to learn how scientists study animals and insects in the rain forest. Ask if any of them know how scientists might do this. Then explain that scientists watch the creatures up close. Scientists look for things that they eat, what they do, and how they spend their days.

Materials Needed for the Class

- jar with lid
- magnifying glass
- live flies or mealworms
- small amounts of dirt
- piece of sponge
- water
- drinking glass
- piece of tagboard or poster board
- Tangled Web Activity Sheets (pages 42 and 43)

Procedure

1. Get the spider's home ready. Place some dirt in the bottom of the jar.
2. Add a small piece of sponge and a twig to the bottom of the jar. Dampen the sponge with water.
3. Punch small holes in the lid of the jar.
4. Catch a spider for his new home. Place only one spider in a jar, please.
5. Look in corners and near the ceiling for a spider. When you find one, put the drinking glass over it and slide the tag/poster board over the glass to trap the spider.
6. Transfer the spider to its new home. Keep the sponge damp and provide food for the spider daily.
7. Spend about 10–15 minutes a day watching your spider. Do this over a period of a couple of weeks. Then the spider can be released if you wish or kept longer.
8. Have the students fill in the Tangled Web Activity Sheet.

Extension

Go to the library and find a book about spiders. Write a story or a poem about spiders. Draw pictures of different kinds of spiders.

Closure

Have students keep a spider diary as part of their journals. Have them write about their spiders daily and explain what is happening with their spiders.

Spying on Spiders *(cont.)*

TANGLED WEB ACTIVITY SHEET

Draw a picture of your spider in its new home.

How does your spider move?

_____

_____

_____

How does it eat?

_____

_____

_____

Spying on Spiders *(cont.)*

TANGLED WEB ACTIVITY SHEET

Does your spider molt (shed its skin)? Explain.

_____

_____

_____

Can you find your spider's eyes? Explain.

_____

_____

_____

How does your spider clean itself? Explain.

_____

_____

_____

Can you tell if your spider is male or female? Explain.

_____

_____

_____

Does your spider lay eggs? Explain.

_____

_____

_____

How do the eggs look? Explain.

_____

_____

_____

Just the Facts

Recent estimates are that 19 to 50 million acres of the rain forest are lost each year due to farming, logging, mining, and other human impact. These human activities have severely disrupted the ecological balance found there. It is important for children to understand that they can do their part to save the rain forests for future generations.

Most South American countries have made an effort to protect the rain forests, but in Central America almost two-thirds of the region's rain forests have been destroyed by the cattle ranching and farming industries.

The once vast jungle regions in Africa have already been destroyed by lumbering and slash-and-burn farming. Slash-and-burn farming consists of cutting away trees and other vegetation from the land and then burning the land to destroy what is left. Then crops are planted on the land. However, the soil is so poor that only two or three crop rotations can be planted in an area before all the soil's nutrients are used.

Logging and clearing for rubber plantations have already destroyed two-thirds of the rain forests in Malaysia and Borneo.

There are efforts being made in many of the rain forest countries to replant the rain forests, but the efforts at reforestation have not been able to make a dent in the damage that is rapidly progressing.

A tropical rain forest is a delicate biological network. Disruption of any of the webs creates an imbalance in the ecosystem. Students should be made aware that if people work together to save the rain forests, one day they could be highly diverse jungle habitats again.

Jungle Journey

Question

How can you make people aware of the ecosystems in the rain forest?

Setting the Stage

- Play a tape of rain forest sounds to set the mood of the jungle. Discuss what sounds you hear and what might have made them.
- Then read *The Great Kapok Tree* by Lynne Cherry to the class. Look at the pictures and list all the animals that are found in the forest.
- Then make rain forest buttons to wear and posters to hang around school.

Materials Needed for Each Group

- construction paper
- scissors
- markers or crayons
- 3" (7.5 cm) cardboard disks
- safety pins

Procedure

1. Determine what facts you want people to know about the rain forest.
2. Write a saying or statement about the rain forest.
3. Draw a picture to go with your saying on a piece of construction paper and ask permission to hang your poster somewhere in the school.
4. Write "Save the Rain Forest" on the cardboard disk and draw a picture to go with your saying. Use a safety pin to attach your cardboard disk to yourself and wear it proudly around school.

Extension

Have the students turn their buttons upside down in a pile. Have the students each chose one and act out the animals on them for the class. The class can guess the names of the animals.

Closure

In your rain forest journal, write a sequel to the story *The Great Kapok Tree.*

Earth Day Quilt

Question

What are the factors that are destroying the rain forest?

Setting the Stage

Ask the students if they have ever celebrated Earth Day. Explain that Earth Day is celebrated on April 22 each year. It is a day that is dedicated to making people aware of the Earth's environmental problems. No matter who we are or where we live, we all call the planet Earth home. You do not have to look far to realize that the rain forests are in trouble. Each day we can search newspapers and watch television to learn of tree cutting and the burning of the rain forests. Since we cannot make everyone in the world aware of the rain forests' problems, we can make our school aware by making a "save the rain forest quilt" for Earth Day.

Materials Needed for the Class

- 10" x 10" (25 cm x 25 cm) squares of felt or white cotton (A white sheet can be cut into squares if felt is unavailable, 1 for each student.)
- fabric crayons, markers, or paints
- colorful yarn cut into 6" (15 cm) pieces

Procedure

1. Pass the squares out to the class. Each student should do his or her own.
2. Have the students design squares that represent a variety of environmental issues and concerns. This can include pollution, destruction of the rain forest, overpopulation, endangered species, and threats to the environment or ways to save it.
3. Collect the squares and tie them together with the yarn in a large square quilt.
4. This step is optional. The quilt can be titled on another sheet of fabric and tied into the quilt in the same manner.

Extension

Additional quilts can be constructed using different themes. Some suggestions are endangered animals, recycling, and conservation.

Closure

Have students write letters to the governments of the rain forest nations, asking them to pass legislation to prevent deforestation of the rain forest. Be sure to provide addresses to students.

Countdown to Action to Save Our Earth

Question

How can we become involved in saving the Earth and its rain forests?

Setting the Stage

- Even though you do not live in the rain forest, there are still many ways that you can save the Earth and its rain forests. You're doing one very important thing right now—learning about the Earth and its rain forests. Educating people about our environment is the first important step in making this a better place to live for all the world's creatures, including you.

- Explain to the students that there are many ways their class can become involved, both at home and in the community. The following activities span 10 days of environmental activities for your class. They may be used anytime during the school year, but they are especially pertinent the 10 days before Earth Day, April 22.

- Read Dr. Seuss's *The Lorax*. Discuss the story and how the events relate to the real-life problems students experience today.

Countdown to Action to Save Our Earth *(cont.)*

Day 10 Activity—Chart Your Course

Materials Needed for Each Group

- chart-size sheet of white paper
- markers or crayons

Procedure

1. Divide the chart paper into three equal parts.
2. Have each group construct a chart with three headings—"PROBLEMS," "CAUSES," and "SOLUTIONS."
3. Put the charts on display in a prominent part of your room.
4. Tell the students that as they proceed with the countdown, they will learn about environmental problems and ways to help solve them.
5. Explain that as they proceed through the countdown, they will be completing the charts.

Countdown to Action to Save Our Earth *(cont.)*

Day 9 Activity—Anti-Litter Bugs

Materials Needed for Each Individual

- construction paper in various colors
- scissors
- markers and crayons

Procedure

1. Have the students create colorful signs for their desks and buttons to wear, both depicting various ways that people litter.

2. Then have the students become aware of litter around school and in the classroom. Encourage them to clean up when paper, broken pencils, or crayons are found on the floor. Outside the classroom, remind students to throw litter in the proper containers and to recycle.

3. Have the students note the environmental problems they found for the day and enter them on their charts.

Countdown to Action to Save Our Earth *(cont.)*

Day 8 Activity—Supply Spies

Materials Needed for Each Individual

- a list of household hazardous wastes

Procedure

1. Tell your students that people use many products every day that cause pollution. For example, many cleaning products contain toxic wastes, such as ammonia, that can contaminate water supplies when they are washed down the drain.

2. Have the students become "toxic waste investigators" and find out if any of the materials used in the classroom contain toxic wastes.

3. Have the students speak with the school custodians about the materials they use around school. Ask the custodians if their supplies contain any toxic wastes.

4. Have the students do some investigating and come up with a list of alternatives that can replace the products with toxic wastes.

5. They can write the results of their findings on their group charts.

Countdown to Action to Save Our Earth *(cont.)*

Day 7 Activity—Plant Power

Materials Needed for the Class

- a variety of cutting or seedlings for the students to plant and care for in the classroom (Some of the best pollution absorbers are philodendrons, golden pothos, and spider plants. These can be found at a local nursery.)
- potting soil
- water

Procedure

1. Discuss the problem of indoor air pollution with your students.
2. Explain that indoor air in some buildings can become polluted because of the pollutants from glues, new carpeting, toxic cleaning products, and other sources can become concentrated inside poorly ventilated buildings.
3. Tell the students that some kinds of household plants absorb certain air pollutants and help improve the quality of air.
4. Have each group of students plant its own pollutant fighter.
5. Explain that they are responsible for the care and watering of their plant.
6. Add this information to the charts.

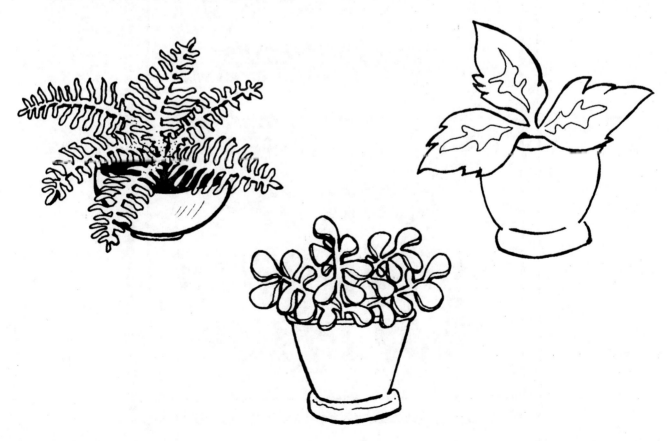

Countdown to Action to Save Our Earth *(cont.)*

Day 6 Activity—Light the Way

Materials Needed for Each Individual

- 3" x 5" (7.5 cm x 12.5 cm) blank index cards
- markers or crayons

Procedure

1. Explain to the students that every time they flick on a light switch or run hot water, they are using electricity and that this electricity use is probably contributing to pollution. That is because large amounts of electricity are produced by coal- or oil-burning power plants which emit harmful materials into the air. Point out to the students that they can help the air by using less electricity.

2. Have the children design eye-catching mini-posters to put next to light switches to remind people to turn off the lights when they are not needed.

3. Have a contest to choose the right poster for your classroom.

Countdown to Action to Save Our Earth *(cont.)*

Day 5 Activity—Lunch Bunch

(This activity requires prior preparation and parental help. A few weeks before "the rain forest feast," contact some parents to prepare lunch for the class. Make suggestions for the types of food to be served or supply a menu and a list of foods.)

Setting the Stage

Ask students to think of foods that might grow in a warm, tropical climate. Explain that many of the foods we eat come from the rain forest. Tell your students that they are going to taste a rain forest lunch. It will surprise many of them to know that some of their favorite foods come from the rain forest.

Materials Needed for the Class

- peanut butter and jelly sandwiches
- assorted nuts and berries—Brazil nuts and cashews
- assorted fruits—mangoes, bananas, papayas
- ice cream
- napkins, plates, utensils
- beverages
- provide students with government addresses for letter writing

Procedure for After Lunch

1. Clean up the lunch area.
2. Recycle any cans or paper goods that are recyclable.
3. Discuss the rain forest feast. Most children will not realize that many of the foods we commonly eat come from plants in the rain forest. Have the children look through books to find more rain forest foods, such as chocolate and coffee.
4. Write to the governments of the rain forest countries to find out more about the crops they grow for export.
5. Show the video *Fern Gully: The Last Rain Forest.*

Countdown to Action to Save Our Earth *(cont.)*

Day 4 Activity—Waste Watchers

Materials Needed for the Class

- 1 roll of paper towels
- copy of "Waste Detective Log" activity sheet (page 55), one per student

Procedure

1. Hold up the roll of paper towels in front of the class. Ask the students if they know where the paper towels come from. Do not be surprised if they answer, "the supermarket." Actually, they are correct, but continue to question the towels' origin, leading the children to answer the rain forest.

2. Continue the questioning by asking if anyone knows how many paper towels are wasted in the classroom. Ask if anyone uses more towels than the job requires.

3. Once it is determined that people waste not only paper towels but, also paper products in general, ask the students to become "waste detectives" and keep a record of all the ways people waste paper. This may be done over several days or weeks if time allows. Have the children write their findings on their Waste Detective Logs.

4. After the time allotted have the children compare their findings. A list or a graph can be constructed so they can visualize the results.

5. Have the students enter the information on their charts and discuss solutions to the paper problem. Ask what other materials could be substituted for paper towel. What ways can we conserve paper?

Some Suggestions

1. Use rags to clean up desks and spills. The students can take turns rinsing them out or taking them home for washing. Discuss sanitation issues of paper towels vs. sponges an cloth, environmental impacts of water and soap vs. industrial strength cleaners, etc.

2. Cut reusable pieces of paper into note-size pads.

3. Use leftover pieces of construction paper for bookmarks.

4. Write on both sides of notebook paper.

Countdown to Action to Save Our Earth *(cont.)*

Day 4 Activity—Waste Watchers *(cont.)*
Waste Detective Log

Waste Watcher	Crime	Solution

Day One:

_____   _____   _____

_____   _____   _____

_____   _____   _____

Day Two:

_____   _____   _____

_____   _____   _____

_____   _____   _____

Day Three:

_____   _____   _____

_____   _____   _____

Day Four:

_____   _____   _____

_____   _____   _____

_____   _____   _____

Day Five:

_____   _____   _____

_____   _____   _____

_____   _____   _____

Countdown to Action to Save Our Earth *(cont.)*

Day 3 Activity—Media Mania

Materials Needed for the Class

- stationery
- envelopes
- pens or pencils
- stamps

Procedure

1. As your class nears the end of the countdown, have the students publicize their achievements in the school and local newspapers.

2. Have the students make posters to alert the public about the deforestation of the rain forest. Call the supermarket to ask them to display the posters. Most community businesses are happy to display children's work.

3. Have the children create an environmental action sheet to distribute to visitors to their school.

4. Contact the local newspaper to ask for a story about your class's efforts to save the rain forest. Most local papers enjoy printing human interest stories, and the children will love seeing their pictures in the paper.

56

Countdown to Action to Save Our Earth *(cont.)*

Day 2 Activity—Check the Chart

Materials Needed for the Class

- posters, notes, logs, and journal entries made during the course of your study of the rain forest

Procedure

1. Have the class review their findings and evaluate the class charts that they have been keeping.
2. Discuss with the students what they enjoyed most about the activities and what they did not enjoy.
3. Look over the class charts and decide whether they solved all the problems listed.
4. Decide what worked and what did not. What projects would you like to continue throughout the school year and which ones should be improved?
5. Decide as a class how you can continue to educate people about the rain forests.

Countdown to Action to Save Our Earth *(cont.)*

Day 1 Activity—Blast Off!

Procedure

Below are some ideas for projects that you and your students might want to take on to help solve environmental problems in the community.

1. Sponsor a community litter pickup. Enlist parents and other classes to spend a day cleaning up the schoolyard or the neighborhood park.
2. Sponsor a school beautification project. Plant trees and flowers around your school to improve the air quality and to make your school more beautiful.
3. Educate the public about the endangered animals in the world.
4. Write to the governments of rain forest nations, asking them to pass laws protecting the rain forests.
5. Publish an alternative cleaning products list for other classes in your school.

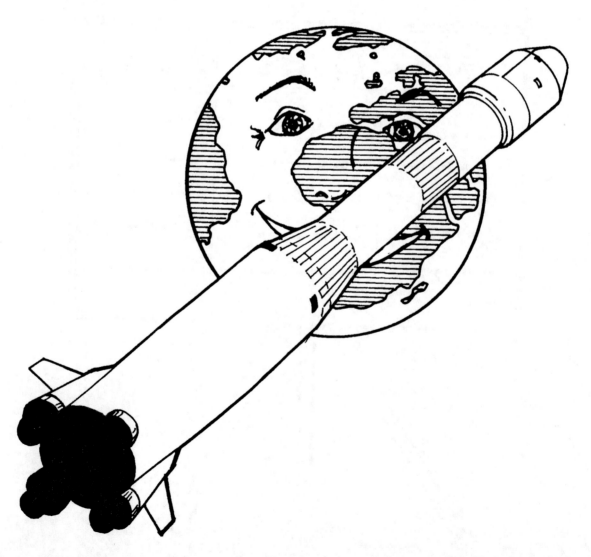

58

Observe

Before you begin your investigation, write your group members' names by their jobs below.

_____Team Leader   _____Stenographer

_____Biologist   _____Transcriber

Read "Natural Selection" below and determine ways that many organisms through time have changed physically (color, body design, beak shape, etc.).

In areas close to your station, time each other for 30 seconds or one minute as each of you tries to locate as many butterfly patterns as you can. Answer the following questions on the back of this paper. (Watch closely, for some may be easier to find than others. Why?) How the does color of an organism help prevent its destruction? Explain. What is meant by *camouflage*?

NATURAL SELECTION

The process of natural selection refers to apparent changes species have undergone through time in order to survive in a dynamic system. For instance, it has been observed that beaks of certain birds have changed in shape and function to suit a changing environment. Also, amphibians are believed to have developed lungs as adults so they could inhabit land in a time when water environments were overpopulated and food was scarce.

"Survival of the fittest" is a scientific theory suggesting that, through time, those species that have survived have adapted to an ever-changing world and those that have become extinct were unable to accommodate change quickly or adequately enough. It is interesting to note that some species such as sharks appear to have changed little over millions of years.

Put your finished activity paper in the collection pocket on the side of the table at this station.

Note to the teacher: Use the butterfly pattern sheet to copy several butterflies of different species and then color them. Place them strategically around the station or center area. Be sure to include some that are strong contrasts to the background and some that are other shades that blend with the background.

Observe *(cont.)*

Copy, color, and cut out butterfly patterns.

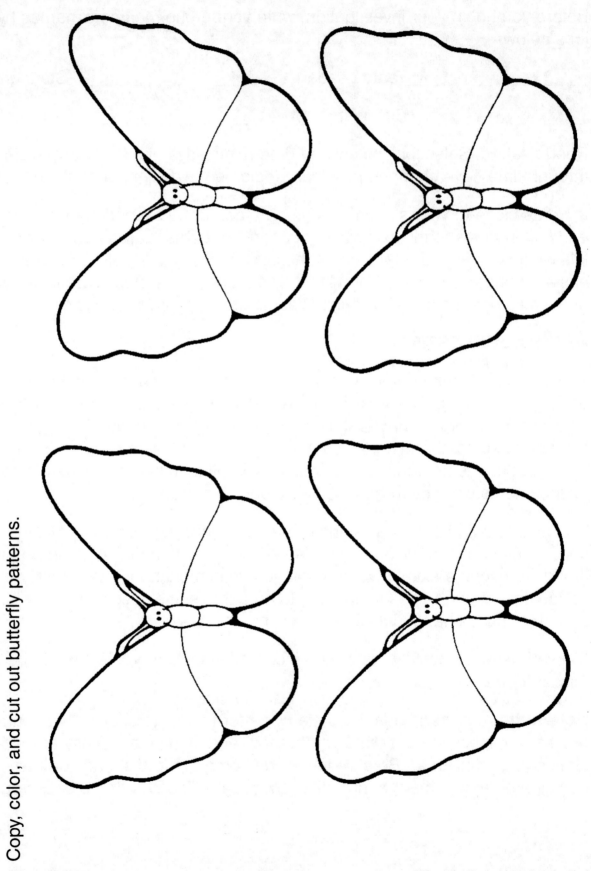

Communicate

Before beginning your investigation, write your group members' names by their jobs below.

_____Team Leader   _____Stenographer

_____Biologist   _____Transcriber

Can you decipher the coded puzzles below? Each puzzle spells out a word describing the eating habits of animals in the wild. Good luck!

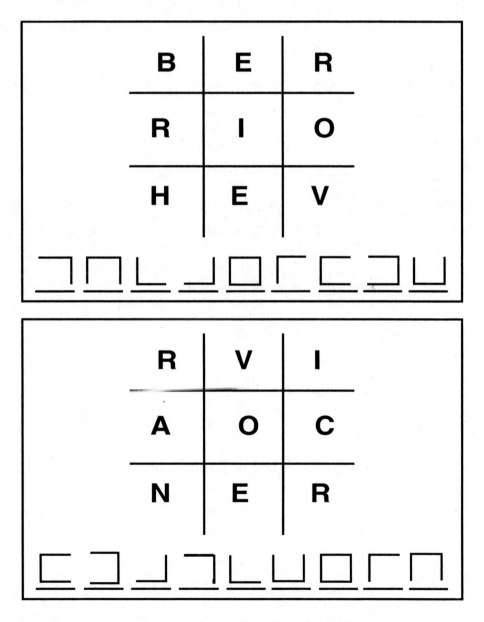

Put your finished activity paper in the collection pocket on the side of the table at this station.

Compare

Before beginning your investigation, write your group members' names by their jobs below.

_____Team Leader   _____Stenographer

_____Biologist   _____Transcriber

Many animals have very acute senses, such as smelling, hearing, and seeing. They have developed these senses over time as a means of survival. For instance, many animals are warned of predators quickly enough to flee because they hear, see, or smell them. Also, many predators would starve if not for their keen senses to help them locate food.

To compare your sense of sight to that of a predator animal, follow the steps below:

1. Test and measure the distance of your limited sight by placing a colored, wooden block 1" x 1" (2.5 cm x 2.5 cm) on the ground.

2. Back away slowly from the block and measure, in yards (meters), the distance you are away from the block when you can no longer see it.

3. Multiply this value by eight. This will give you the distance at which predator birds such as eagles can detect their prey.

4. How far were you able to back up before you could no longer see the wooden block?_____

5. How far away can an eagle see the block?_____

Now you see why an eagle is such a great hunter!

Put your finished activity paper in the collection pocket on the side of the table at this station.

Order

Before beginning your investigation, write your group members' names by their jobs below.

_____Team Leader   _____Stenographer

_____Biologist   _____Transcriber

In the food pyramid below, organize each level according to its particular function or role. Begin by arranging, in order, the list of species provided. Complete by drawing and labeling each species in its appropriate placement or level on the food pyramid.

> hawk, spider monkey, toucan, arrow poison frog, boa, morpho butterfly, jaguar, tarantula, green plant leaves, three-toed sloth, tapir, humans

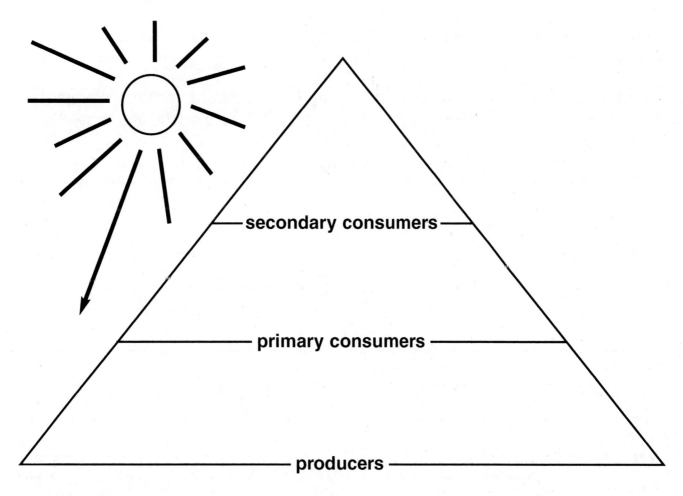

Put your finished activity paper in the collection pocket on the side of the table at this station.

Categorize

Before beginning your investigation, write your group members' names by their jobs below.

_____Team Leader   _____Stenographer

_____Biologist   _____Transcriber

There are living and nonliving things in this world. Living things are plants, animals, insects, and bacteria. These living organisms are all made up of cells. They require food, water, and air to survive. Most living things are able to move or get around. Some accomplish this with limbs, fins, or wings. Most living organisms also must obtain food. Some catch their food, some make their own food using light energy from the sun, and some get their food by absorbing nutrients from the earth or decaying things.

Nonliving things are things that do not need food, water, or air to survive. These things are made from atoms. They are solids, liquids, or gases. Examples include rocks, soil, plastic, glass, cement, and metals.

As you take a tour of your schoolyard or your own backyard, look for examples of living and nonliving things. List them below and describe why you think they are one or the other.

LIVING

NONLIVING

Put your finished activity paper in the collection pocket on the side of the table at this station.

Relate

Before beginning your investigation, write your group members' names by their jobs below.

_____Team Leader   _____Stenographer

_____Biologist   _____Transcriber

Match the picture of the living organisms below with the statement telling why they are endangered.

Some people like to wear boots or belts made from my skin.

People keep clearing us and decreasing our numbers in order to make room for more and more people.

During history, humans have overhunted us at an alarming rate. For a while, we were almost gone forever.

Humans have feared us throughout history and have conquered us to prove their superiority.

Many people like us for our soft, warm fur, even though there are many products for sale that can do the same job.

Put your finished activity paper in the collection pocket on the side of the table at this station.

Infer

Before beginning your investigation, write your group members' names by their jobs below.

_____Team Leader   _____Stenographer

_____Biologist   _____Transcriber

In the year 1800 the world's population was one billion people.
In the year 1900 the world's population was two billion people.
In the year 2000 the world's population will be six billion people.

Graph this information on the chart below.

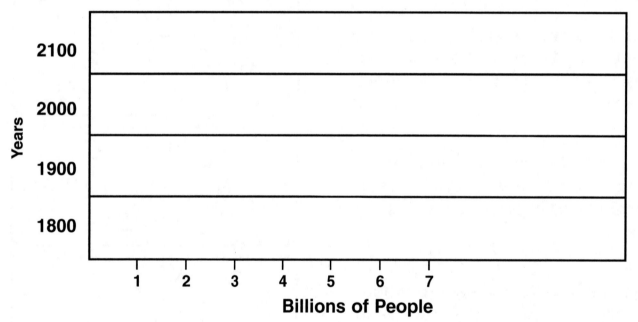

1. Based on your graph, what do you predict the world population will be in another 100 years?_____

2. Why?_____

3. Use a new color to graph your prediction above.

Put your finished activity paper in the collection pocket on the side of the table at this station.

Apply

Before beginning your investigation, write your group members' names by their jobs below.

_____Team Leader   _____Stenographer

_____Biologist   _____Transcriber

When I am escaping from a predator, I squirt dark ink at my enemy. For a moment this confuses him and he loses track of me. For the short time that he cannot see me, I slip away safely. Who am I?

> I am a_____, and I live in the_____.
> I have many predators, such as_____and
> _____. My favorite food is_____.

I hang out in large groups of my own kind. You know what they say—"There is safety in numbers." If one of us becomes alerted to danger, we all become alerted. Our numbers will always be fairly high because our natural predators can't get us all.

> I am a_____, and I live in the_____. I
> have many predators, such as_____and
> _____. My favorite food is_____.

I cleverly disguise myself or blend in with my natural environment as a way of fooling my enemies. If I remain perfectly still, they might go right by me without being aware of my presence. Soon they will give up, and I can be on my way.

> I am a_____, and I live in the_____. I
> have many predators, such as_____and
> _____. My favorite food is_____.

Put your finished activity paper in the collection pocket on the side of the table at this station.

Apply *(cont.)*

To scare my predators, I make them think that I am bigger and scarier than I really am. I have markings on my wings that are big and round. When I open my wings, my enemies think they are seeing a big head with large eyes.

I am a_____, and I live in the_____.
I have many predators, such as_____and
_____. My favorite food is_____.

As a class, make up the next two together or work in groups and try to stump your friends or other classmates. Be sure to describe a creative and/or unique adaptation or behavior of a plant or animal that makes it special. Have fun!

I am a_____, and I live in the_____.
I have many predators, such as_____and
_____. My favorite food is _____.

I am a_____, and I live in the_____.
I have many predators, such as_____and
_____. My favorite food is _____.

Put your finished activity paper in the collection pocket on the side of the table at this station.

Animal Information Cards

Guide to Using the Cards

Pages 69–78 are filled with Animal Information Cards. These boxes may be mounted on colored construction paper and be placed on the classroom walls. Pages 80–82 have the corresponding Animal Illustration Cards. These may also be mounted and displayed adjacent to the appropriate Information Cards.

The Animal Information and Illustration Cards can also be used in a matching game. For example, post the information cards around the room. Read the descriptions, one at a time, to the class. Allow one student to match the correct illustration to the Information Card.

These cards can provide an excellent, initial resource if you are having your students do animal research reports. At the end of this section, there are some blank cards for other rain forest animals.

Challenge: The following are challenge questions and activities related to some selected animals on the Animal Information Cards. You might use these as extra credit, quiz questions, or discussion starting points.

Parrots: Research how parrots can be bred humanely in captivity. Would you buy for a pet a parrot bred this way? Why or why not?

Harpy Eagle: Being a predator, the harpy eagle is an integral part of the balance of nature in the tropical rain forest. What do you think would happen if this predator became extinct?

Sloth: If a sloth moves through the branches at only one-half mile per hour, how long would it take for him to travel to the next cecropia tree six miles away?

Jaguar: Compare and contrast the plight of the jaguar with that of the leopard.

Chimpanzees: Write a commercial for a tool from a chimp's point of view. Perform your commercial for your class.

Quetzal

The quetzal of Southern Mexico and Central America is among the most beautiful birds in the world. The quetzal is also known as the royal bird of Costa Rica. Its body is green with highlights of gold and red. The black wings of the quetzal have splashes of white on them. The male quetzal is about 15 inches (38 cm) in length from head to tail. However, the long wisp of feathers beneath its tail add another 15 to 30 inches (38 to 76 cm) to the quetzal's length. The female quetzal is slightly less attractive. Her feathers are not as vibrant in color nor are her feathers as long and graceful as her male counterpart's.

Quetzals are known to eat ants and wasps, but they mainly depend on the fruits of the wild avocado tree for nourishment. The quetzal is an endangered animal because excessive logging of the rain forest has resulted in the loss of many wild avocado trees.

The quetzal's great beauty has inspired people to incorporate it into their cultures in many ways. Often, rain forest native art and mythology have featured this royal bird. The ancient Mayans and Aztecs considered the quetzal to be a sacred creature. Today, the quetzal serves as the national symbol of Guatemala.

Animal Information Cards *(cont.)*

Macaw

Macaws are the world's largest parrots. There are several different kinds of spectacularly colored macaws, and they all live in South America. Macaws are seed predators rather than seed dispersers. They are able to eat the toughest fruits and seeds, even if they contain toxic chemicals.

Macaws have large, powerful bodies which protect them from being eaten by many bird predators. The macaw's hooked beak can open even the hardest nuts, like Brazil nuts, with ease. It uses the edge of the beak like a saw to cut partially through the shell, making it easy to complete the job. The top and bottom parts of the macaw's beak constantly rub against each other, keeping the edges sharp.

The macaw's beak is also useful as an extra foot when climbing through the trees. The macaw's foot has four toes. Two of these face forward, and two of them face backward. This enables the macaws to pick up objects and hold them tightly.

Parrots such as macaws make popular pets and are often taken into captivity. Although there are laws attempting to protect the parrots, poachers continue to illegally capture and sell these beautiful creatures.

Toucan

Some of the most distinctive birds that come from the tropical rain forests are toucans. Toucans have large, brightly colored beaks which are serrated and are displayed in courtship rituals. Toucan beaks are so large that they are sometimes longer than the toucan's body!

There are about 37 species of toucans, the largest of which is the Ramphastos. In general, the toucan's body is usually one to two feet (30 to 60 cm) in length. The plumage of these birds matches their personalities; both are very loud. Sections of the vibrant colors such as red, yellow, and green contrast sharply with the mostly black or dark green feathers on the toucan's body. These colorful birds are supported by strong legs and feet which have two toes pointed forward and two toes pointed backward.

Toucans nest in the tree cavities of the Central and South American rain forests. In these nests, both toucan parents incubate and raise their offspring. Fruit makes up the bulk of the toucan diet.

Animal Information Cards *(cont.)*

Harpy Eagle

The topical rain forest is the home to the world's largest and most ferocious eagle, the harpy eagle. This rare predator hunts high up in the jungle canopy. It sleeps at night and hunts by day. The harpy eagle is a very swift and agile flyer which enables it to chase monkeys through the jungle. Its gray feathers provide the eagle with a natural camouflage.

The harpy eagle makes its nest in the tallest emergent trees (most often the silk-cotton trees). Usually only one harpy eagle chick is successfully raised on the large platform of twigs used as a nest. It takes six months for the chick to reach adulthood.

The harpy eagle dines mainly on unsuspecting, sleeping sloths and chattering capuchin monkeys. Occasionally, their diet includes agouti, kinkajous, snakes, anteaters, large parrots, and small deer.

Caiman

Caimans are reptiles that are closely related to their Central and South American neighbors, the alligators. Adult caimans are usually four to six feet (1.8 m) in length. They have short legs and powerful tails which are used for both swimming and as weapons.

Caimans live along riverbanks where they patiently wait for thirsty animals to come for a drink—then, they attack their unsuspecting prey! They can float under the water with only their eyes, nostrils, and ears showing. A valve closes off the gullet of the windpipe so that the mouth can be opened under water to eat its favorite food—fish. The caiman's greatest enemy is man.

Some Caimans' have been found to leave the river to lay their eggs next to termite nests. As the termites continue to build their nests, they surround the caimans' eggs. The nests keep half the eggs warm and half the eggs cool. The warm eggs develop into male caimans, and the cool eggs develop into females. When the baby caimans hatch, they head straight for the river where they spend their lives.

Animal Information Cards *(cont.)*

Gorilla

Because gorillas are the largest living primates, they are quite often misunderstood. They are usually represented as aggressive, violent, and short-tempered creatures, when in fact they are actually one of the most gentle primates in existence. These giants of the African rain forests can reach up to six feet (180 cm) in height and 400 pounds (180 kg) in weight. Despite their size, fighting among the gorillas is rare.

Contrary to popular belief, the gorillas are not carnivores (meat eaters), but rather they are herbivores (plant eaters). During the daytime they forage for food on the forest floor. Unlike other members of the ape family, most gorillas, due to their size, do not scour the treetops in search of food or shelter.

Gorillas live and travel in family groupings. The family unit consists of one dominate silverback male (the term "silverback" comes from the gray fur on a mature male), one or two females, a few young males, and various juveniles. Gorillas are quadrupeds because they travel on all four limbs. They use the knuckles of their "hands" to help support their heavy upper bodies.

Tarsier

The tarsier lives in the rain forests of Indonesia, Malaysia, Brunei, and the Philippines. This Southeast Asian mammal is in danger of extinction because its forests are being destroyed. The tarsier is a rat-sized relative of the monkey.

This creature is one of the strangest looking primates, in large part because of its unique eyes, ears, and feet. Its body is only about six inches (15 cm) in length. The tarsier has long, powerful hind legs which allow it to leap up to 20 feet (6 meters). The pads on its toes and fingers help it hold on to branches. The tarsier's head can almost turn in a complete circle. This is a very important feature, since the tarsier cannot move its eyes.

This animal spends most of its life living in the trees of the rain forest. It is, for the most part, nocturnal (active during the night and resting during the day), and it has large, sharp eyes that enable it to hunt all sorts of small animals at night. It leaps onto its prey (which is usually a lizard or an insect), catches the creature with its "hands," and then kills it with its sharp teeth.

Animal Information Cards *(cont.)*

Fer-de-Lance

The most feared poisonous snake found in Central and South America is called the fer-de-lance. This snake gets its name from the Creole-French language, and it means "head of a lance." A lance is a type of weapon that has a spearhead which some people believe looks similar to the head of this snake. The fer-de-lance averages four to six feet (1.2 to 1.8 meters) in length but can grow up to seven feet (2.1 meters) long. Usually olive or dark brown in color, it has a pattern of dark-edged triangles on its skin.

Small depressions on its head mark a heat-sensing organ that helps the animal find its warm-blooded, mammalian prey by the heat the prey generates. The fer-de-lance protects itself by striking its enemy. Its venom quickly produces severe hemorrhaging and is lethal.

This snake lives in the understory or on the forest floor, hiding among the leaf litter, tree roots, and buttresses. It gives birth to live offspring and may produce as many as 70 young at one time.

Boa

Boas are nonpoisonous snakes. They kill their food by wrapping themselves around an animal and squeezing tightly until the animal dies from suffocation. Boas then stretch their jaws open extremely wide to swallow their prey whole. They are able to open their jaws so wide that they can actually swallow animals that are larger than their own heads.

There are about 70 species in the boa family which can be found worldwide. Unlike some other types of snakes who lay eggs, the boa gives birth to live offspring. Some kinds of boas never grow any longer than 24 inches (61 cm), while others, such as the boa constrictor, may grow as large as 14 feet (4 meters) in length.

One of the most beautiful snakes found in Central and South America is the emerald tree boa. Its green skin is striped with white or yellow, which camouflages it well in its home in the canopy layer. This protective coloration allows the snake to approach its prey without being seen and also helps it to avoid being eaten by its predators, one of which is the harpy eagle.

Animal Information Cards *(cont.)*

Lemur

Lemurs are distant cousins of monkeys. They are found only on the island of Madagascar. They have been able to survive there because of a lack of monkeys on the island that would be competing for the same food.

There are 15 different kinds of lemurs in Madagascar. Most of them are cat or squirrel-sized, but some, like the mouse lemur, are as small as five inches (12.7 cm) long and weigh only two ounces (56 g). The indri lemur is the biggest lemur, growing to over two feet (61 m) long. It is able to make extraordinary leaps through the trees but, when on the ground, bounces on its big back legs.

Most lemurs roam the forest in small groups looking for food. They eat fruit, leaves, bark, and insects. Different types of lemurs are active during different times of the day. Some species are nocturnal (active at night), some are diurnal (active during the day), and some are active only at dusk.

The lemur population is dwindling. Some species of lemurs are in danger of extinction because the forests of Madagascar are rapidly being destroyed.

Aye-aye

The cat-sized aye-aye is an unusual and rare type of lemur. Its enormous eyes and rounded, hairless ears indicate that the aye-aye is nocturnal (it comes out at night). During the daytime it sleeps in hollow trees or among branches. The aye-aye is a very small animal, measuring only about 36 inches (.91 m) long; more than half of that length is due to its bushy tail.

The aye-aye is a loner. It hunts alone, using its long fingers to scoop out bamboo pith, sugar cane, beetles, and insect larvae. The curved, slender fingers are also used to comb its fur. Unfortunately for the aye-aye, the natives of Madagascar believe that these long fingers possess magical properties and bring good luck to the owners. Many aye-ayes have lost their lives because of this—their fingers did not bring them good luck!

Aye-ayes can be found only on the island of Madagascar, and there are fewer than ten aye-ayes known to exist there. Aye-ayes are not found in any of the world's zoos; therefore, the only way we will probably ever view one is to see its picture in a book.

74

Animal Information Cards *(cont.)*

Orangutan

Orangutans can be found only on the islands of Borneo and Sumatra in Southeast Asia. They were named "men of the woods" because their faces are so human-looking. Orangutans are wonderful climbers and spend most of their time in the treetops, swinging from branch to branch.

Like other apes, orangutans do not have tails. They have long red hair and strong arms. Their long toes help them grip the branches as they climb in the trees.

Orangutans have huge appetites. Their favorite food is fruit, but they will also eat leaves, shoots, tree bark, and, occasionally, birds' eggs. Orangutans are very clever and have learned to follow fruit-eating birds to find their favorite food.

The orangutans have become very rare due to the loss of their habitat, the rain forest. Additionally, orangutans have been hunted, captured, and sold as pets. Special reserves have been set up to help the remaining orangutans survive.

Indian Elephant

Indian elephants are the largest animals in the rain forests of Asia, although their African cousins are larger. Elephants roam about in small herds. Their diet mainly consists of leaves, which they pull from the trees and shove into their mouths by using their trunks.

The Indian elephant's two very large teeth are called tusks. These tusks consist of ivory. The females usually have smaller tusks than the males. Unlike the flat back of the African elephant, the Indian elephant has a strongly arched back. It has a domed forehead and a smooth trunk. It can weigh up to six tons (5.44 tones). The ears of the Indian elephant do not reach down as far as its mouth and are smaller than the ears of the African elephant.

Indian elephants have been trained as workers in the forests. They are better than machines when it comes to getting out big logs from between the trees. They can drag huge logs from the forest and pick them up with their trunks and tusks. The forests where they live are gradually being destroyed, and the irony of it is that the tamed, working elephants are helping to cause the damage.

Animal Information Cards *(cont.)*

Anteater

This tree-living, cat-sized anteater is also called a tamandua. It has short, coarse fur and a prehensile tail. South American tamanduas have honey-colored coats, while the Central American ones have bold, two-toned black and tan coats.

The tamandua has powerful claws that help it both in climbing and in getting food. It wraps its tail around tree limbs to hold on while it rips open ant and termite nests with its claws. It then catches the insects with its long sticky tongue, licking up thousands at one time. It also will eat other insects such as bees and beetles.

Contrary to common belief, the anteater does not eat all types of ants or termites! It avoids army ants because they are too aggressive and can sting. It also will not eat leaf-cutter ants, as they are spiny and difficult to swallow in its long, toothless mouth. Azteca ants are a favorite of the tamandua, but the anteaters approach these nests very cautiously. After several minutes of eating these Azteca ants, thousands more of them pour out from the nest, covering the tamandua and biting it with their tiny jaws, causing the tamandua to retreat.

Agouti

The agouti is a large, rabbit-sized rodent with a short tail and long legs. It is mainly active by day (diurnal) but is also active at dusk or at night (nocturnal). It lives on the forest floor and sleeps in burrows.

Agoutis have a very strange behavior called scatter-hoarding. Most rodents destroy all the seeds that they gather and eat; the agouti, however, carries seeds long distances and buries them whole.

There are some trees that produce seeds that are too heavy to be dispersed by bats or monkeys and have to rely on animals like agoutis for dispersal. Brazil nut fruits fall to the ground where their hard, woody shells are chiseled open by the agouti.

The agouti eats some of the seeds and scatter-hoard the rest. They do not usually find all the Brazil nut seeds that they bury; consequently, these seeds germinate and grow into new Brazil nut trees.

Animal Information Cards *(cont.)*

Sloth

The sloth does nearly everything upside down. Found in Central and South America, this slowest-of-all-mammals' top speed is one-half mile per hour. It lives its entire life in one cecropia tree, hanging by its huge hook-like claws. In addition to cecropia leaves, it eats flowers, fruit, and insects.

Its long, coarse, grayish-brown fur grows from its belly towards its back (the opposite of all other animals' fur), which enables the rain to run off easily, keeping the sloth dry in the wet rain forest. Nonetheless, its fur often appears a greenish color due to the algae that grow on it. In addition to the algae, the sloth's fur contains sloth moths, beetles, and mites. When the sloth descends to the forest floor, these insects utilize the sloth's dung to lay their eggs. Caterpillars also live on the sloth's fur and feed on the algae.

The sloth spends nearly its entire life among the tree's branches. It visits the forest floor about once every week or two to defecate, thereby fertilizing its own home. Once on the ground, the sloth cannot walk and must drag itself. However, during the rainy season, when the Amazon floods, sloths can swim from treetop to treetop.

Jaguar

The rarely seen jaguar is the largest predator of the dense forests of Central and South America. The jaguar is an excellent swimmer and climber and usually can be found close to water, where it sleeps by day and hunts by night (a nocturnal animal). It prefers to eat large animals like wild pig or tapir, but, being an excellent hunter, its diet also includes sloths, snakes, mice, caimans, turtles, iguanas, and fish. The jaguar is the major predator of the lower levels of the rain forest.

The jaguar's coat is spotted like its cousin's, the leopard, but its rings are different. Nearly all of them have a spot in the middle. This camouflages the jaguar as he stalks through the jungle. Jaguars can weigh up to three hundred pounds (136 kg).

A number of disasters threaten these beautiful creatures. Jaguars have long been hunted for their luxurious fur. Although there are many laws protecting these creatures, illegal killing and smuggling of the jaguars' fur continues. As the human population grows, rain forest land is being slashed and burned to clear land for ranching. This is causing a loss of habitat for many rain forest animals which the jaguar depends upon for food. Consequently, the jaguars have begun to feed on the ranchers' livestock. In turn, this has resulted in their being killed by the ranchers.

Animal Information Cards *(cont.)*

Chimpanzee

Scientists believe that of all wild animals, chimpanzees are our closest relative. Chimpanzees make their homes in the rain forests of Africa. They have been known to live in groups of up to 100 animals. The noisiest male is usually the group leader. Male chimpanzees often fight with one another. Female chimps are friendlier and get along well. Male chimps grow to be about five feet (1.52 m) tall and weigh about 110 pounds (50 kg). Female chimps are usually a little smaller. Chimps, like other apes, do not have tails.

Chimpanzees eat plants and meat. They are capable of killing pigs and antelope for food. Male chimps work in teams to trap monkeys in trees. When they are lucky enough to find a large amount of food, the males make drumming noises on the tree trunks to call other chimps to the feast.

Chimpanzees are very clever. They have learned how to use simple tools to get the food they want. They use sticks to crack nuts to get the juicy kernels inside and to catch tasty termites. Chimps have also been known to chew leaves, making them spongy, so they can use them to soak up water for drinking.

_____

(animal)

_____

_____

_____

_____

_____

_____

_____

Blank Cards

_____
(animal)

Animal Illustration Cards

Quetzal

Macaw

Toucan

Harpy Eagle

Caiman

Gorilla

Animal Illustration Cards (cont.)

Tarsier

Fer-de-Lance

Boa

Lemur

Aye-aye

Orangutan

Animal Illustration Cards *(cont.)*

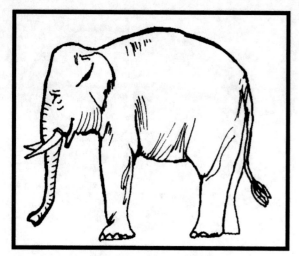

Indian Elephant

Anteater

Agouti

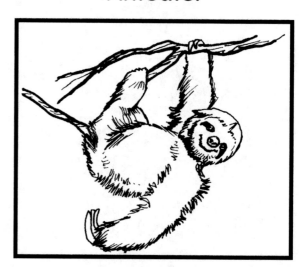

Sloth

Jaguar

Chimpanzee

Science Safety

Discuss the necessity for science safety rules. Reinforce the rules on this page or adapt them to meet the needs of your classroom. You may wish to reproduce the rules for each student or post them in the classroom.

1. Begin science activities only after all directions have been given.

2. Never put anything in your mouth unless it is required by the science experience.

3. Always wear safety goggles when participating in any lab experience.

4. Dispose of waste and recyclables in proper containers.

5. Follow classroom rules of behavior while participating in science experiences.

6. Review your basic class safety rules every time you conduct a science experience.

You can have fun and be safe
at the same time!

My Rain Forest Journal

Rain forest journals are an effective way to integrate science and language arts. Students are to record their observations, thoughts, and questions about past science experiences in a journal to be kept in the science area. The observations may be recorded in sentences or sketches which keep track of changes both in the science item or in the thoughts and discussions of the students.

Rain forest journal entries can be completed as a team effort or an individual activity. Be sure to model the making and recording of observations several times when introducing the journals to the science area.

Use the student recordings in the rain forest journals as a focus for class science discussions. You should lead these discussions and guide students with probing questions, but it is usually not necessary for you to give any explanation. Students come to accurate conclusions as a result of classmates' comments and your questioning. rain forest journals can also become part of the students' portfolios and overall assessment program. Journals are valuable assessment tools for parent and student conferences as well.

How to Make a Rain Forest Journal

1. Cut two pieces of 8.5" x 11" (22 cm x 28 cm) construction paper to create a cover. Reproduce page 85 and glue it to the front cover of the journal. Allow students to draw rain forest pictures in the box on the cover.
2. Insert several Rain Forest Journal pages. (See page 86.)
3. Staple together and cover stapled edge with book tape.

My
Rain Forest
Journal

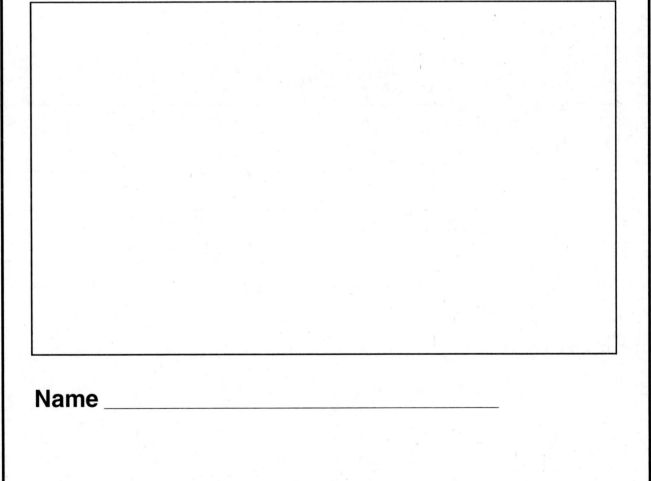

Name _____

My Rain Forest Journal

Illustration

This is what happened: _____

_____

_____

_____

_____

This is what I learned: _____

_____

_____

_____

_____

My Science Activity

K-W-L Strategy

Answer each question about the topic you have chosen.

Topic: _____

K—What I already **know:** _____

_____

_____

_____

_____

W—What I **want to find out:** _____

_____

_____

_____

_____

L—What I **learned after doing the activity:** _____

_____

_____

_____

_____

Investigation Planner

Observation

_____

_____

Question

_____

_____

Hypothesis

_____

_____

Procedure

Materials Needed:

_____

_____

_____

_____

Step-by-Step Directions (Number each step.):

_____

_____

_____

_____

_____

_____

Rain Forest
Observation Area

In addition to station-to-station activities, students should be given other opportunities for real-life science experiences. For example, a mini-computer and terrarium can become vehicles for discovery learning if students are given enough time and space to use and observe them.

Set up a rain forest observation area in your classroom. As children visit this area during open work time, expect to hear stimulating conversations and questions among them. Encourage curiosity but respect their independence!

Assessment Form

The evaluation form below provides student groups with the opportunity to evaluate the group's overall success.

Cooperative Group Evaluation

Assignment: _____

Date: _____

Scientists	Jobs
_____	_____
_____	_____
_____	_____
_____	_____

As a group, decide which face you should fill in and complete the remaining sentences.

1. We finished our assignment on time, and we did a good job.
2. We encouraged each other, and we cooperated with each other.

3. We did best at _____

_____

4. Next time we could improve at _____

_____

Super Biologist Award

This is to certify that

_____

Name

made a science discovery.

Congratulations!

_____

Teacher

_____

Date

Super Biologist

Glossary

A

adaptation—Changes in the behavior or structure of plants or animals that enable them to survive in their surroundings.

agroforestry—A land-use system in which trees and crops are grown alongside each other. This maintains the forest as a self-renewing resource.

algae—A group of simple plants that usually live in wet and damp places. Many of them are very small.

anthropologist—A person who studies the physical and social characteristics of mankind.

B

biodiversity—Many different kinds of life in one area.

biome—The largest type of ecological unit, characterized by a distinctive set of plants and animals maintained under the climactic conditions of the region. Examples include deserts and tropical rain forests.

bromeliad—A tropical plant that grows on the branches or trunks of trees. It is a member of the pineapple family.

buttress—A fan-shaped bottom on some of the tall rain forest trees that helps hold the tree upright.

C

camouflage—The way in which animals avoid the attention of their enemies by resembling or blending in with their surroundings.

canopy—A thick, overhead layer of the rain forest formed by the branches and leaves of the tall trees.

carbon dioxide—A colorless gas that is formed by the combustion and decomposition of organic substances. Carbon dioxide is absorbed from the air by plants in photosynthesis.

cash crops—Agricultural products, such as coffee or bananas, that are sold for profit, often by export, rather than raised for consumption by the producer.

clear cutting—Removing all the trees in a forest, leaving an open patch.

conservation—Protection of natural resources from waste or loss or harm.

D

decomposer—Organisms, such as bacteria, fungi, and many insects, that break down dead plant and animal materials to be recycled and used by the living.

deforestation—The destruction of a forest. In the tropics, deforestation is caused by a number of activities, such as slash-and-burn agriculture, cattle ranching, and timber harvesting.

development—The alteration of the environment for the benefit of human beings.

diurnal—Refers to animals that are active during the day and rest at night.

drip tips—Leaves that come to a point, allowing rainwater to drip off.

Glossary (cont.)

echolocation—The ability of an animal such as a bat or a dolphin to orient itself by the reflection of the sound it produces.

ecology—The study of the environment and the relationship of organisms to it.

ecosystem—A community of animals, plants, and microscopic life that interact in a particular place in the environment.

emergent—The layer of trees in the rain forest that tower in height above others and receive the most sunlight. They can grow to be 300 feet (91 meters) tall.

endangered species—An animal or plant that is threatened with extinction.

environment—All the physical surroundings that are around a person, animal, or plant.

epiphyte—A plant that grows on another plant but does not harm it.

equator—An artificial circle that splits the earth into the northern and southern hemispheres.

erosion—Washing or wearing away of soil.

ethnobotanist—A researcher who studies native plants and their use by the local, indigenous peoples.

exploitation—To use for some purpose for one's own advantage or profit at someone or something else's expense.

extinction—The permanent loss of an animal or plant species.

food chain—The flow of energy (food) among different groups of organisms in a natural community.

forest floor—The bottom layer of the rain forest.

global—A term pertaining to the planet Earth, meaning worldwide or universal.

greenhouse effect—The trapping of heat by the air around the earth.

habitat—An area that provides enough food, water, shelter, and space for an organism to survive and reproduce.

humidity—The amount of water vapor in the air.

hunter-gatherers—People who get most or all of the food they need by hunting and by gathering wild plants.

indigenous—Growing or living naturally in a particular region or environment. The term "indigenous people" is used to mean tribal people.

invertebrates—A group of animals that have no backbone.

jungle—A general term which is interchangeable with the term "tropical rain forest."

Glossary *(cont.)*

N

nature reserve—An area set aside to protect wild plants and animals, often rare ones, that are in danger of becoming extinct.

nectar—A sugary fluid secreted by plants to attract pollinators.

nocturnal—Refers to animals that are active at night and rest during the day.

nutrients—Substances such as vitamins and minerals that are necessary for life.

O

organic—Of plant or animal origin.

ozone layer—The region of concentrated ozone that shields the earth from excessive ultraviolet radiation.

P

parasite—An organism dependent upon another living organism for support or existence.

photosynthesis—A process in which plants convert carbon dioxide into water and sugar.

pollen—Powder-like microspores produced by the flower, containing the male sex cell.

pollination—The transfer of pollen from the male reproductive organs to the female in seed plants.

R

rain forest—A very dense forest in a region, usually tropical, where rain is very heavy throughout the year.

reforestation—The action of renewing forest cover by planting seeds or young trees.

S

seed dispersal—The way that seeds travel from the parent plant to the ground by wind, gravity, or animals.

slash-and-burn agriculture—The method of agriculture in which people clear land by cutting down patches of forest and burn the debris.

species—A group of organisms that have the same traits and can produce offspring that can also produce offspring.

sustainable development—Development that uses natural resources in an efficient way and without destroying the basis of their productivity. It allows natural resources to regenerate.

T

threatened species—Any species of indigenous plant or animal that could become endangered in the near future if the factors causing its population decline are not reversed.

tropical—Hot, humid zone between the Tropic of Cancer and the Tropic of Capricorn.

tropical rain forest—An evergreen forest located at low elevations in regions between the Tropic of Cancer and the Tropic of Capricorn. Tropical rain forests are characterized by abundant rainfall and a very warm, humid climate year round.

U

understory—The layer growing under the canopy. This layer is comprised of shrubs, herbs, and young trees.

Bibliography

Academic American Encyclopedia. *Jungle.* Vol.11, Groiler Inc., 1986.

Althea. *Rainforest Homes.* Cambridge U Pr., 1985.

Burnie, David. *How Nature Works.* Reader's Digest, 1991.

Cherry, Lynne. *The Great Kapok Tree.* Harcourt Brace Jovanovich, 1990.

Chinery, Michael. *Rainforest Animals.* Random Books Young Readers, 1992.

Cooper, Sally Ann and Cradler, Carolyn. *General Science.* Media Materials, 1988.

Costa de Beauregard, Diane. *Animals in Jeopardy.* Young Discovery Library, 1991.

Cuthbert, Susan. *Endangered Creatures.* Lion USA, 1992.

De Vito, Alfred and Krockover, Gerald. *Creative Sciencing.* Scott, Foresman and Co., 1991.

EarthWorks Group. *50 Simple Things Kids Can Do To Save The Earth.* Scholastic Inc., 1990.

Farndon, John. *How The Earth Works.* Reader's Digest Association, 1991.

Frank, Majorie. *202 Science Investigations.* Incentive Publications, 1990.

Giant Book of Questions and Answers. Octopus Publishing, 1990.

KIDS Discover. *Rain Forests.* KIDS Discover, 1993.

Melton, Lisa and Ladizinsky, Eric. *50 Nifty Science Experiments.* Lowell House, 1992.

Morris, Dean. *Endangered Animals.* Raintree Steck-V, 1990.

National Wildlife Federation Staff. *Endangered Species.* National Wildlife, 1991.

Ontario Science Centre. *Scienceworks.* Addison-Wesley Publishing Co., 1986.

Parks, Mary. *"Making An African Rainstick."* Instructor Magazine, Jan./Feb., 1995.

Reader's Digest. *ABC's of Nature.* Reader's Digest Association, 1984.

Schwartz, Linda. *Earth Book For Kids.* The Learning Works, 1990.

Stone, Lynn. *Endangered Animals.* Childrens, 1984.

Toleman, Marvin. *Earth Science Activities for Grades 2–8.* Parker Publishing, 1986.

Tropical Rain Forests of the World. The Book People, 1990.

Uchitel, Sandra & Serge Michaels. *Endangered Animals of the Rain Forest.* Price Stern, 1992.

Van Cleave, Janice. *Earth Science For Every Kid.* John Wiley and Sons, 1991.

Van Cleave, Janice. *200 Gooey, Slimy, Weird and Fun Experiments.* John Wiley and Sons, 1993.

Wapole, Brenda. *175 Science Experiments to Amuse and Amaze Your Friends.* Random House, 1988.

Bibliography *(cont.)*

Spanish Titles

Bornemann, E. *¡Nada de tucanes!* (No Toucans Allowed!). Lectorum, 1987.

Cowcher, Helen. *La tigresa* (Tigress). Farrar, Strauss, & Giroux, 1993.

Suess. *El Lorax* (The Lorax). Lectorum, 1993.

Wright, Alexandra. *¿Los Echaremo de Menos? Especies en peligro de extincion* (Will We Miss Them? Species in Danger of Extention). Charlesbridge Publishing, 1993.

Technology

Cornet. *Animals of the World Series: Animals of a Living Reef, Animals of North America, and Animals of South America.* Available from Cornet/MTI Film & Video, (800)777-8100. video

Inview. *A Field Trip to the Rainforest.* Available from Sunburst, (800)321-7511. software

National Geographic Series. *STV: Rain Forest.* Available from VideoDiscovery, (800)548-3472. videodisc

Orange Cherry. *Talking Jungle Safari.* Available from CDL Software Shop, (800)637-0047. software

Partridge Film & Video. *Monkey Rain Forest.* Available from Cornet/MTI Film & Video, (800)777-8100. videodisc